STAYING SAFE AT SCHOOL

STAYING SAFE AT SCHOOL

WHAT YOU NEED TO KNOW

Chester Quarles

CERTIFIED PROTECTION PROFESSIONAL

BROADMAN
&HOLMAN
PUBLISHERS

NASHVILLE, TENNESSEE

0-8054-2421-0

Dewey Decimal Classification: 371.7
Subject Heading: SCHOOL VIOLENCE—UNITED STATES—
PREVENTION / SCHOOLS—SECURITY MEASURES—
UNITED STATES / SAFETY
Library of Congress Card Catalog Number: 00-031231

Unless otherwise stated all Scripture citation is from the New
King James Version, copyright © 1979, 1980, 1982, Thomas
Nelson, Inc., Publishers.

Library of Congress Cataloging-in-Publication Data
Quarles, Chester L.
    Staying safe at school / Chester Quarles.
        p. cm.
    Includes bibliographical references.
    ISBN 0-8054-2421-0 (pbk.)
    1. School violence—United States—Prevention.
2. Teachers—Crimes against—United States—Prevention.
3. Schools—Security measures—United States. I. Title.
    LB3013.3 .Q38 2000
    371.7'82'0973—dc21

                                            00-031231
                                            CIP

1 2 3 4 5 04 03 02 01 00

Dedication

To my wife, Dot, and our children, who have
completed their education,
and to my grandchildren, who have not:

Christopher, Rachael, Rebekah, Joseph, Hannah,
Benjamin, Mac, Joshua, Chyna, and Annalee.

May this book teach them the skills to avoid, deter,
prevent, and survive crime.

Note from the Author

There isn't a fundamental conflict between street-crime prevention and basic Christian practice. The Scriptures clearly demonstrate the security approaches God recommended for his people. *Staying Safe at School: The Life You Save May Be Your Own* focuses on these issues without apology.

While you won't find profanity or vulgarity in these pages, you will find "straight" talk. While it is harmful to inappropriately label other teenagers, in the crime-avoidance profession, we must describe them appropriately. The words *bully, troublemaker, doper, outlaw, crackhead, gangster, creep, thief, prostitute,* and *pervert* are descriptive of certain forms of sinful behavior. Herein is just one of many conflicts. It is easy, almost glib, to state that Jesus witnessed to thieves, robbers, prostitutes, and murderers before he witnessed to the religious people of his day. I believe that Christians should minister to all of those in need. But while we should ordinarily not be rude to those considered to be undesirable, the average Christian youth doesn't always have the wisdom or spiritual insight to deal with them effectively.

The risks this book approaches are those in school, at school, going to school, returning from school, and at school-related activities. I will never recommend that you restrict your witness. Teens who personally know the Master enjoy the "peace that passeth understanding." They walk forward in faith, with Jesus.

There is another problem. Assertiveness and aggression are discouraged in many Christian homes, but these are often the qualities you need to avoid criminal attack. Courtesy is not one of the Ten Commandments; nor is there a Scripture stating, "Thou shalt not be rude." I'm not asking you to be discourteous under normal circumstances, but if people who give you the creeps are bothering you, you have permission to be discourteous.

Don't be afraid of fear. Look at fear like an "Angel of God" sitting on your shoulder—whispering, shouting, or even screaming the word BEWARE. As you read this book, carefully consider the Scripture references and ask the Lord to lead you down the pathway he chooses for you. Yes, you should let others see Jesus in you. You should radiate the quality of his love, His compassion, and his focus, but you should not be "Pollyannish." Pollyanna thought that nothing bad would ever happen to her. Bad things do happen to good people, believers and witnesses alike, but they don't have to happen to you—if you obey God's crime-prevention rules.

Chester L. Quarles, Ph.D., CPP

Table of Contents

Introduction

Although schools often look like they are safe, appearances can be deceiving. Crime is frequent, and it causes more disruption than ever before. School is where young people and teenagers go to be disrespected, bullied, assaulted, robbed, and raped. Violence is a serious threat to education. Some schools have high crime rates because they are located in high-crime areas, but many schools *are* the crime problem for the community.[1] Children are shot, stabbed, and murdered each day—most often by other youth. In the U.S. about fifteen youth under the age of nineteen are murdered each day.[2] Almost 75 percent of youth murders are the result of gunfire.[3]

"Recent studies indicate that more serious crimes are being committed at school and the age at which crimes are being committed is increasingly younger and the frequency of child and teen assaults is increasing."[4]

Eighty-three percent of all youth twelve years of age or older will become victims of actual or attempted violence during their lifetime according to the U.S. Bureau of Justice Statistics.[5] Many factors are used in studying crime. One significant factor is *age*. Age is an element of victimization you can't control. You are either young, middle-aged, or older, but *the younger you are, the greater your risk.*

In 1993, 116 preschoolers died by gunfire in the U.S.—more than the number of police officers or American soldiers killed in the line of duty during that same time span.[6]

The statistics are staggering. More American young people have been killed by guns in the last thirteen years than were killed in Vietnam. Every year since 1950, the number of American children killed with guns has doubled. Every two days, twenty-five kids, the equivalent of an entire classroom, are murdered.[7]

Americans are at the greatest risk of becoming crime victims during their teenage years. In 1992 almost one in every four violent crimes involved a victim aged twelve to seventeen. Teenagers are more than twice as likely to be victims of violent crimes than those over twenty.[8]

Young children should be taught about crime and criminals as soon as they can understand. By the time a child leaves home for kindergarten, the child should have crime-avoidance training. The purpose of the training is not to make the child distrustful but to help the child avoid crime and criminals. Most parents discover that a child who develops crime-avoidance habits at an early age will keep these habits throughout adolescence and on into adulthood. Young people need to understand crime-avoidance approaches, both in what they should do and what they must do to lower the chances that they will become a victim.

Recent School Shootings

DATE	PLACE	RESULTS	
May 26, 2000	Lake Worth, FL	1 dead	no injuries
Mar. 23, 2000	Lisbon, OH	Held class hostage at gunpoint, no dead	no injuries
Mar. 10, 2000	Savannah, GA	2 dead	1 injury
Feb. 29, 2000	Mt. Morris Township, MI	1 dead	no injuries
Dec. 6, 1999	Fort Gibson, OK	no dead	5 injuries
Nov. 19, 1999	Deming, NM	1 dead	no injuries
Apr. 20, 1999	Littleton, CO	15 dead	20 injuries
Apr. 16, 1999	Notus, ID	no dead	no injuries
June 15, 1998	Richmond, VA	no dead	2 injuries
May 21, 1998	Springfield, OR	2 dead	22 injuries
		Parents were killed as well.	
May 21, 1998	St. Charles, MO	Police prevented this attack.	
May 21, 1998	Onalaska, WA	1 suicide	
May 21, 1998	Houston, TX	Accidental discharge, 1 injury	
May 19, 1998	Fayetteville, TN	1 dead	no injuries
Apr. 28, 1998	Pomona, CA	2 dead	no injuries
Apr. 24, 1998	Edinburo, PA	1 dead	no injuries
Mar. 24, 1998	Jonesburo, AR	5 dead	10 injuries
Dec. 1, 1997	West Paducah, KY	3 dead	5 injuries
Oct. 1, 1997	Pearl, MS	2 dead	7 injuries
		In addition, this shooter killed his mother before school.	
Feb. 19, 1997	Bethel, AK	2 dead	no injuries
Jan. 27, 1997	West Palm Beach, FL	1 dead	no injuries
Feb. 2, 1996	Moses Lake, WA	3 dead	1 injury

Change the Circumstances of Your Crime

Staying Safe at School will teach you about crime and violence. It will show you how to perform a "risk assessment" to determine if you should feel threatened. Some teenagers are unnecessarily frightened. Others are blissfully unaware of the incredible danger facing them each day. This book will also show you how to lower your risk and increase your safety; how to recognize the troublemakers and to prevent trouble; what to do in a crisis and, more importantly, what *not* to do. If your crime-avoidance plan fails and you become a victim, this book will also show you methods to improve your chances of survival.

Potential victims of many crimes can drastically reduce their risk of victimization by making changes in their lifestyles. If you follow the strategies recommended in this book, your chances of being victimized by predators will be considerably reduced, both at school and in the community.

There are very few random crimes. Most are planned. You can't stop the plan, but you can change the circumstances, forcing criminals and delinquents to alter their plans. You can alter the likelihood of "your" assault. A teenager who avoids the more dangerous areas of the school, who walks with friends, who develops crime-avoidance partnerships, who is friendly to all, and who avoids conflict is less likely to be attacked. Staying in public view deters virtually every type of crime. All attacks can't be stopped; but any action that increases the difficulty of an assault or decreases the likelihood of the criminal getting away is effective.

Facing Your Fear

This is also a book about facing fear. It is a book about moral, physical, and spiritual courage. Courage is not the absence of fear; it is the control of fear.[9] This book is *not* about fighting, karate, judo, physical defense, mace, pepper spray, or the use of weapons. In truth, your safety level *decreases* when anyone takes a weapon to school; but if you do what this book says, you will be safer. You will learn how to work with other students, teachers, and administrators to increase the safety of all. By applying what you learn from this book, you can decrease your chances of criminal attack while protecting yourself and assisting others as they avoid crime.

The Scriptures Show Crime-Prevention Approaches Too

The book will also help you avoid and deter crime while serving Christ. Some believers feel that Christians should *always* be passive. Others believe the only example Christ gave the contemporary believer was to "turn the other cheek." We will examine the Scriptures carefully to ensure that the crime prevention and avoidance methods we use will pass the standards established in the Bible.

In your home, school, and community, you will be safest when you are centered in and focused on spiritual values established by God. These standards and values in themselves are trouble-avoiding mechanisms. Sometimes, however, a teenager is threatened because of a Christian standard. The threat may occur when the biggest, meanest, and most abusive bully at your school insists that you write his homework assignment. While you may not object to helping him, you know that it is unethical to let him turn in your work as his. So you have a problem—and if your bully is really big and mean, you have a big problem. *Staying Safe at School* will show you how to deal with your bully.

Don't look at the Scriptures as if they are just used in Sunday school and other worship services. The Bible is much more than a book of worship and praise. It can be used to help you walk confidently and securely forward in genuine faith within the will and the power of a mighty, loving, protecting God.

My hope is that you will learn how to prevent, deter, and avoid crime and grow in knowledge both of the Scriptures themselves and the Lord who gave them to us.

chapter 1

Are You Afraid?

Jimbo Lane and his sister, Katie, saw Billy, a local teenage tough, attack a ten-year-old kid right after school. Billy hurt the little boy. They reported the incident and gave the principal the bully's name. Somehow Billy figured out who told on him, and now he is harassing the Lanes. A really big fellow, he has already shoved Jimbo down a flight of stairs; and he touched Katie while making coarse sexual remarks. He says that he has just begun to get even with them for "messing with him." The intensity of Billy's attacks on Jimbo and Katie is increasing.

Jimbo and Katie are frightened and don't know what to do. They are also concerned about their mom. A single parent, their mom already has a lot of problems; and they don't want her to be worried about their safety too. However, if the assaults get any worse, Jimbo will be visiting the hospital emergency room, and Katie will be raped.

So far the attacks are without witnesses. Katie hasn't told Jimbo about Billy touching her because she is afraid he will fight Billy. Jimbo's a lot smaller, so he could most certainly lose. All she's told him is that Billy has harassed her and she's scared. They're both afraid. What should they do? What should they *not* do? They decided to discuss their options with their youth pastor. During Katie and Jimbo's meeting with their youth pastor, Katie talked more openly about her experiences, including Billy's sexual advances.

The youth pastor advised them to tell their mother everything, even the sexual touching part, which is very embarrassing for Katie. Then, along with their mother, they made an appointment to meet with the school principal. Billy has been a real troublemaker for quite some time, but very few complaints have been made against him from students, probably because they were afraid of him. This time, however, he had gone too far. The principal decided to transfer Billy to an alternative school where his behavior could be more closely supervised. He thanked the Lane family for coming forward with the information he needed to document the transfer. Billy was not even told of these specific complaints. He was just told that he had misbehaved too often to remain.

National Survey Shows Fear Level at School

One recent national survey of middle- and high-school students conducted by the National School Safety Center discovered that over eight hundred thousand young people stay home at least once a month because they are afraid to go to school.[1] This figure includes about 8 percent of the entire school population.[2] They don't "play hooky" to watch a soap opera or to go fishing. They stay home because they want to keep their dignity, their Nikes, the same clothes they went to school in, their homework, or their lunch money. They just don't want to be *dissed* (disrespected), so they stay home from school.

Fear is the primary concern of all students according to one recent national study.[3] Since 89 percent of all school crime is committed by other students,[4] many students are afraid to go to school.[5] Serious crimes occur at school. One national survey showed that the risk of robbery is greater in school than out,[6] and another showed that 7 percent of all the violent acts committed at school involved the crime of rape.[7]

Fear of other students is the reason one out of every twelve students reports for dropping out of school.[8] These students are literally "pushed out" of school by violence, intimidation, and fear. They didn't drop out.[9]

Chances are that you've been afraid, too, or you wouldn't have picked up this book. If the title of this book attracted your attention, then you're afraid, or at least concerned about your safety at school. Maybe you're scared to death—some teenagers even get sick to their stomach because they are so frightened. Others are so tense, they shake! Sometimes the fear is a theological problem as well as physical or emotional.

We all must confront our fears. In Psalm 23 David wrote, "Yea, though I walk through the valley of the shadow of death, I will fear no evil; For You are with me" (Ps. 23:4). God doesn't want believers to be incapacitated by fear. He promises to be with us and not forsake us as we walk with him. The Bible and this book can show you how to avoid crime and how to demonstrate courage.

This book is about "people-fear," where strangers, older students, gang members, bullies, or drug pushers frighten you. It also addresses fears about fists, gangs, drugs, knives, and guns. Five out of six of today's twelve-year-old children will be the subject of violence as serious as felony assaults, robbery, rape, or murder.[10] Half of these will face violence twice.[11] Homicide is the leading cause of death among African-American males aged fifteen to nineteen years and the second leading cause of death for all youth.[12] The Children's Defense Fund projected that an American child is fifteen times more likely to be killed by gunfire than a child living in Northern Ireland.[13]

Many parents believe that gun-wielding, violence-prone students are a product of the last few years, but this is incorrect. Nationwide, between September 1986 and June 1990, at least 75 people were killed with guns at school, over 200 were wounded, and at least 243 were held hostage at schools by gun-wielding assailants.[14] The carnage continued into the late 1990s as Eric David Harris and Dyland Klebold murdered twelve other students and a teacher, and injured twenty-three in a spree killing, before committing suicide.

Spree killers shoot indiscriminately, although some of their victims are carefully selected. These victims are shot first, and the shooters kill until they are satisfied with their violence, run out of bullets, or are arrested. However, it is not just the spree-killer students who are taking guns to school. The Children's Defense Fund studied this problem in 1991 and estimated that 135,000 children bring guns to school every day.[15] A more conservative study in 1993 by the largest American teachers' association predicted that one hundred thousand children carry guns to school.[16] The word *children* is used because some kindergartners, first graders, and those in other elementary school grades are also bringing guns to school.

Even if you aren't afraid for yourself, maybe you are afraid for your little brother or sister. Are you afraid for a friend who is weaker or less assertive than you? Are you concerned about the safety of your boyfriend or girlfriend? Test your fear level. The truth is, fear levels are increasing; more middle- and high-school students are afraid. (Interestingly enough, junior high or middle schools are more dangerous than lower- or higher-grade schools.[17]) Private interviews and questionnaires clearly demonstrate that the teenager fear level is higher than it was three years ago.

Males between the ages of fifteen and seventeen commit most juvenile offenses, and delinquent behavior decreases after age seventeen.[18] Victims can't control the age factor. You are either young or old, and you can't grow any faster. The younger you are, the greater your risk. Younger persons' risk is nearly eight times higher than the risk for older adults.[19] Students are often afraid to go to school.

Sometimes you tell your parents about your fear, but it is likely your parents don't relate to your situation. When they grew up, gangs were relatively harmless, just groups of kids "goofing off" and maybe getting into occasional trouble. Every school had its bullies.

Drugs were not so easily accessible when your parents attended school, and assault weapons were less sophisticated and more difficult to obtain. Today, assault weapons are often purchased *at* school. In many cases, the school *is* the neighborhood weapon store. Count all the guns and knives at your school. You may determine that an arsenal is already there. Maybe this book will help you to "open up" and discuss the safety and security issues that you face at school and in your community. Talk—communicate—with your parents, school officials, and church youth leaders about these issues. Let them know how you feel and what you are observing.

The Most Dangerous Place You Go Is School

Your parents often do not understand that your school is the most dangerous place you go. Usually parents are concerned most about the mall, the movie theater, the bowling alley, or the youth game rooms. Statistical studies show that their concerns are appropriate but perhaps misplaced. The fact is, you are more likely to become a crime victim *at school* than anywhere else.[20] Moreover, about 8 percent of the nation's schools have a serious crime problem.[21]

The most dangerous school is junior high, or middle school. Assaults and robberies are twice as great in junior high schools as in senior.[22] Freshman and sophomore students commit more crimes at school than those in other classes.[23]

Approximately 282,000 students are physically attacked in America's secondary schools each month.[24] Including these attacks, there are nearly one-half million shakedowns, robberies, and attacks each month.[25] The figures, however, don't show the complete problem. School crime affects more than just the victim and

---

CONSIDER THESE FACTS

- Juveniles commit nearly one-third of all serious crime in the U.S.A. (FBI, Uniform Crime Report).
- The school-age population includes the primary criminals in the U.S.A. Nearly 50 percent of all police arrests involves the school-age population (National Institute of Education, 1978).
- In the average street crime, juveniles are eight times more at risk than adults. The younger you are, the more your risk (*Danger From Strangers*, 39).
- Murder by firearms is the number one cause of death for African-American males and the second leading cause of death for all young American males (Center to Prevent Handgun Violence in America).
- If you are in the age range from ten to twenty, you are fifteen times more likely to be murdered than your parents (*School Safety 101*).
- Over 40 percent of all crimes against young people occur at school! (The National School Safety Center).
- No one, regardless of age, race, sex, or economic status is free from the threat of physical assault (Brewer, 6).

---

the school criminal. It affects the whole school, the educational atmosphere, and the morale of all who attend. Teenagers become distrustful, fearful, angry, frustrated, and increasingly rebellious in a dangerous environment.

According to the National Center for Education statistics, many of our public schools are "no longer safe places of learning."[26] According to the National School Safety Center, at least 40 percent of all crimes against children and teenagers occur at school.[27] Since you spend only about 25 percent of your total waking hours at school, the school crime rate is disproportionate. The truth is: *the most dangerous place for a young person is school.*

Parents often give advice based on their own experiences. In discussing a bully, many fathers will tell a teenage son, "If you fight back, he will pick on someone else." Your parents' experiences were quite different, however. In their youth, students usually fought with their fists. The end result was a skinned knuckle, a black eye, or a sore mouth. Usually, the worst injury required dental work.

Today, however, many school-age criminals and gang members bring guns and knives to school. *U.S. News and World Report* reported April 6, 1998, that approximately 20 percent of all high school students regularly carry a firearm, knife, razor, or club to school. While this is probably an overstatement, there is no doubt that many students bring weapons to school. Today's fight ends with broken bones, slashed arteries,

---

The most dangerous place for a young person is school (National School Safety Center).

Risk of assault and robbery to urban youngsters aged twelve to nineteen is greater in school than at any other location (Vestermark and Blauvelt, 7).

stab wounds, bullet holes, paralysis, and death. Fighting should always be the last option on your list of alternatives. Fighting with weapons should never be an option.

What Would the Lord Have You Do?

The Lord is sovereign. He is in control. We are commanded to live faithfully within his will. Life is not going to be easy because we are children of the most high God. Contemporary Christians must prepare for adversity just as the early believers did. We must be faithful, and we must follow the examples set in the Scriptures. We often let the secular world influence our spiritual world. It is very easy to be influenced by the latest video game or "shoot 'em and leave 'em" movie, but this is not Christ. This is not Christianity.

As we search the Scriptures for guidance and wisdom, we can study many verses to help us. These include the Scriptures concerning Saul as he attempted to murder young David and the verses relating to the persecution of the prophets. Many of the prophets fled to the hillsides, lived in caves, and hid themselves from those who would kill them.

Probably the apostle Paul set the best examples for Christian survival. He urged Christians to "put on the whole armor of God" (Eph. 6:11). Paul was threatened by the Jews or by Roman authorities frequently. Oftentimes he defied them, but he was still careful about safety matters. Only by surviving could he continue to share the gospel of Christ. At Damascus Paul "was let down in a basket through a window in the wall, and escaped" (2 Cor. 11:33). At Iconium he and Barnabas *fled* (Acts 14:6). They *left* Lystra for Derbe after being stoned (Acts 14:6–19). At Thessalonica he and Silas *hid and ran away during the night* (Acts 17:10). Jason, a believer, had harbored them and they were then *asked to leave by the Christian brethren* (Acts 17:7–10). When Paul left Greece, *he avoided an assassination plot by changing pre-planned routes of departure* (Acts 20:2–3).

These are all scripturally approved crime-prevention, crime-deterrence, and crime-avoidance approaches. You certainly have biblical permission to use the same approaches. These verses are God's "guide" for your crime-deterring and crime-prevention behavior. You are *not* a coward when you follow scripturally approved crime-avoidance methods. It is not necessarily wrong to hide. It's not necessarily wrong to withdraw or to move your residence. *Target denial* is the term used by police and security professionals. Move out of harm's way.

Maybe you should go live with your aunt across town or in another city altogether. Maybe God wants you to change schools, so that your enemy's "target" is no longer where he wants it. By moving, running away, or changing your schedule (to avoid him altogether), you have denied him the target.

You must also be careful about what you believe. Making Christ the Lord of your life does not give you a God-ordained heavenly immunity, protecting you from the trials and troubles of this world. There is no "spiritual safety" umbrella protecting you from the perils of your own poor decisions, even when you are focused on spiritual priorities. Just remember the persecution and perils of the apostle Paul.

This great servant of God was beaten five times with a whip, twice with rods; stoned; shipwrecked (staying in the water a night and a day); attacked by the Jews and heathen; and had perils in the city, in the wilderness, and at sea. He was often weary and in pain, hungry, thirsty, and cold, and even naked on occasion (2 Cor. 11:24–27).

The Bible does not promise that Christ, or his angels, will protect you in everything you do. It particularly does not say that he will protect you when you are involved in unacceptable conduct, are visiting inappropriate locations, or are involved in ungodly pursuits. The Bible does not say Christ will protect you if you do something stupid. Even if you are a member of the family of God, you still must use the instinct, intuition, knowledge, skill, and logic that God has given you to use for his earthly kingdom.

You Can Make a Big Difference

You can make a difference at your school. You can be Christ's witness there. You can influence your school, your neighborhood, and your home. First of all, remember that you are not alone and you are not without resources. You are not powerless. You have a lot of personal influence if you will just step in, step up, and speak out. The safest schools in America are the best schools, offering the best training and teaching. Students in safe schools succeed in English, math, and science instead of the three "disruption Rs" (rape, robbery, and rebellion, or reading, writing, and razor blades). Schools with good teachers have a good learning ratio. Their students score well on national examinations and college entrance exams. Kids who have a desire to go to college can continue their education.

Good students and good teachers enjoy safer schools. You, personally, make a difference in safety when you do your best in each of your classes, avoid clowning around or other disruptions, and obey the reasonable requirements set forth at your school.

c h a p t e r   2

Crime Prevention

Bobby is concerned about crime at his school. He has
seen several criminal assaults, and some of the victims
left school in an ambulance. He's even seen girls
abused there. Bobby is a big, strong fellow himself, so
the bullies and the gangsters leave him alone. He is
really concerned about some of his friends, however,
and he is worried about his little brother, Joey. What
can Bobby do to help? Can he get together with other
students and the faculty to decrease the violence? Yes,
he can! Just as Bobby is aware of the crimes at school,
others must learn of it too. You can talk to your parents, your church leaders, or your pastor about this
issue. By exposing the truth that you are not safe at
school, students and faculty can work together successfully to lower the violence, substance abuse, and
crime levels. The following chapter will show you
how.

Crime Prevention Can Be Accomplished by Almost Anyone

Crime prevention can be very simple. It is any approach that protects the potential victim from harm. The first requirement is that a potential victim must be *alert* to his surroundings. The second requirement is that the potential victim must also be *aware.* By being aware of a threat or by anticipating a possible attack, the potential victim reduces or even eliminates a crime opportunity.

The New Testament gives many strong examples of this response. The apostle Paul was aware that the Jewish leaders wanted to kill him. In fact, almost all of his mission trips were to the Gentiles. He had been forewarned on several occasions about plots to murder him. In each case he responded appropriately. "And when the Jews plotted against him as he was about to sail to Syria, he decided to return through Macedonia" (Acts 20:3). By listening to threat-related information, Paul changed his travel plans. In changing his plans, he probably saved his life.

Later Paul was taken into protective custody by Roman soldiers in Jerusalem because a group of Jewish zealots threatened his life. He was spared a whipping (scourging) because he revealed that he was a Roman citizen (Acts 22:25–29). The Roman centurion gave him safe passage out of Jerusalem when the zealots persisted in their threats against Paul.

Another time, a group of more than forty extremists banded together and vowed that they would not eat or drink until they had killed Paul (Acts 23:12–13). Paul's sister's son heard of the ambush plot

and told Paul (Acts 23:16). Because of his Roman cit-
izenship, the Roman centurion gave Paul two hundred
soldiers, seventy horsemen, and two hundred spear
men to take him to Caesarea at the third hour of the
night (Acts 23:23).

What can the modern-day Christian learn from
this? First, you can see that Paul used every resource
available to ensure his safety. He used personal informants, his sister's son, the authorities, and the quiet
hours of darkness. He slipped away in the wee hours of
the morning while his enemies slept. You can do as
much. It is not wrong to tell the authorities when you
are being threatened, and it is not cowardly to avoid
physical risk. Notice, too, that Paul became actively
involved in his risk-avoidance plan. He prayed daily,
but he didn't just ask God to send a legion of angels.
He was careful in his daily activities, and he listened
to the advice of other believers and even nonbelievers
who were in governmental authority.

Crime-prevention strategy is like a road map. If
you want to travel from one city to an unknown location, you will need a map. The map shows you the best
routes. So it is with a risk-avoidance strategy or a security plan. By following your plan, you are safer than
the individual who has not planned.

Crime Reduction

Certain ingredients are necessary for a crime to take
place. It's like a recipe. If any of the crime ingredients
are missing, there is no crime. Influencing these
"ingredients" lowers your risk.

CRIME INGREDIENTS

- *Desire* on the part of the criminal
- *Skill* on the part of the criminal
- *Opportunity* to commit the crime

There is very little you can do about criminal desire. Some kids are thieves just as some adults are. They want what others have even if they have enough. While you can't change their minds, their ethics, or their desire, you can dress in ways that minimize their desire to steal the things you have. A $20 pair of tennis shoes is much less desirable than a $300 pair of Nikes. A reasonable quality value store jacket purchased for $28 will keep you warm in the winter, but it is much less likely to be coveted than a $400 wool and leather Starter jacket. It is highly improbable that the thief would try to

> Dressing inexpensively can save your life!

steal the $20 tennis shoes or the $28 jacket. Dressing inexpensively can prevent a robbery. It can even save your life because you avoided the very robber that could kill you.

Likewise, it is difficult to influence a criminal's skill. He is an experienced crook or he isn't. He learns by doing. He has a lot of experience at crime, or he has little or none. Even if he is experienced, however, you can lower your risk by increasing his. This can be accomplished by using the buddy system or by traveling in groups with other teenagers. The tough bully or thief is less likely to challenge the group. He would prefer to catch one teenager all alone.

Opportunity is the last area of influence. You decrease the criminal's opportunity when you dress in less expensive clothes and when you travel in a group. You decrease criminal opportunity when you use a safer route through your neighborhood. At night, you reduce opportunity by staying near the edge of the sidewalk and walking under the streetlights rather than taking shortcuts through dark alleys.

Our national government's response to skyjacking is a formidable example of *opportunity reduction.* Back in the 1970s revolutionaries frequently skyjacked airplanes filled with passengers, but you rarely hear about sky-jacking today. Why? Skyjacking is rare today because of opportunity reduction. Sky marshals, security check-points, metal detectors, and bomb-detecting dogs have lowered the risk considerably. Revolutionaries don't sky-jack as much because we have reduced their opportunity to do so successfully. The number of crimes will also be reduced as criminal opportunity is lowered.

What Do the Scriptures Instruct?

I don't want you to become cynical, and I certainly don't want to frighten you further, but the Scriptures are very specific. You should develop a healthy sense of suspicion! This is scriptural—not paranoia. Jesus said in Matthew 10:16: 'Behold, I send you out as sheep in the midst of wolves. Therefore be wise as serpents and

By understanding *how* criminals operate in your town and knowing *where* they operate and *at what time* they operate, you can reduce your risk opportunity.

harmless as doves.' You should develop a good eye for deception. Certainly you don't want to create a world of safety in your mind; one that doesn't exist in reality. Realize that there is good in the world but that crime coexists with the good. Read the newspaper headlines. Read the crime section of your newspaper. Look at the nightly news on television or listen to a radio newscast daily. Read your Bible every day. You will reaffirm the real need for street and school survival skills through your Scripture study.

In his letter to the Philippians, Paul exhorted the believers in the early church to "Do all things without complaining and disputing, that you may become blameless and harmless, children of God without fault in the midst of a crooked and perverse generation, among whom you shine as lights in the world" (Phil. 2:14–15). See the world as it is, not the world you would prefer. Sin destroyed the perfect world and we were left in mortal danger. Danger is all around us, but most American teenagers fail to see it until it is too late. Middle-class Christian teenagers are often naive and trusting. We believe that our institutions are "safe," but often our safety is not real; it is a product of imaging. Safety exists only in our minds. Even in the midst of danger, however, we are to set good examples, letting our spiritual lights shine as Paul described.

Never be lulled into security complacency. Just because nothing bad has happened over the last week or two doesn't mean that a crime won't occur soon. If you want to survive, you not only must play the criminals' game; you must play it better than they do. The Scriptures again tell you what to do! You must be as wise as a serpent and harmless as a dove since you are like a sheep among wolves (Matt. 10:16).

If someone gives you the creeps or you feel the hair on the back of your neck standing up, avoid that person. If you get the creeps at a particular location, do your best to avoid that site. *Listen to your feelings!* Watch, look, and listen. Don't let anyone else talk you out of those feelings. Don't talk yourself out of those feelings either. "Often, when something is wrong, you get a feeling about it. We call this 'listening to your gut.' It's an important warning signal. Many times our instincts know we're in danger before our minds do. When you get a bad feeling about a place or a person, don't ignore it. Leave the place; get away from that person, do whatever you have to do to be safe."[1]

The Crime "Opportunity" Model

The crime opportunity model indicates that your risk increases when you are exposed to criminals. Your risk continues to increase in the absence of capable guardians. Most young people are never victimized before they attend school. Why? Their mom, dad, or an older family member were usually with them when they were younger. It is only when they start school

---

THE CRIME OPPORTUNITY MODEL

- A motivated *offender*
- A suitable *target*
- The *absence* of guardians

and are truly alone that no one is there—no adult, no guardian—to intervene on their behalf.

The Four Elements of Crime

Some criminologists focus on the elements of the crime as well as other related issues. Some claim that four elements are inherent in every crime, rather than just three. First, a violation of the law must take place. It is against the law to steal, to burn a building, to harm someone else, or to kill. For an event to be a crime, it must be against the law coded in your state, county, or city law book. Some laws relate to issues that are evil, like murder, arson, or rape. Other laws refer to offenses like not paying taxes, possessing illegal drugs, speeding, or running stop signs.

The second element of every crime is the victim. A robber takes money from his or her victim. The arsonist burns down a building owned by an individual, a

---

THE FOUR ELEMENTS OF EVERY CRIME

- *The act itself.* A crime is an act made punishable by law.
- *The victim.* You can learn to avoid crime and behavior that increase your chances of victimization.
- *The criminal or the violator.* It is hard to deal with the criminal once the crime is in motion.
- *The place.* This is where you can change things because you control or at least influence your own personal space.

> You can considerably lower your chances of ever being a crime victim. You must know, however, that it is your responsibility to prevent a crime from happening to you.

corporation, or a governmental unit. If someone steals your car or robs you at gunpoint, then you are the victim. Victims can do a lot of things to influence their risks, so you will need to work hard to prevent your own crime.

The third element of every offense is the criminal. Law enforcement officers call the crook a perpetrator, or use the abbreviation PERP. It is hard to influence a PERP (this is a good name for a sorry, contemptible thief or a bully). One reason thieves steal is because they don't have to pay for goods or services when they do. However, we can build in "crime barriers" to make it harder for criminals to commit crimes.

The fourth element of every crime is the place. The place can be crime free, or it can be a nightmare. Schools can lower their risk factors. Your school can deter criminals by locking all but the front door during school hours. This creates a choke point for all visitors and intruders. Some call this activity *access control.* Access control is just one form of environmental crime prevention, or Crime Prevention Through Environmental Design (CPTED). Everyone must gain entrance through this door. Usually the guest entrance is adjacent to the principal's office. Visitor badges are obtained here. Intruders or those who do not have legitimate business at the school are turned away.

Most schools benefit from some form of environmental crime control. The long hallways are open and

easily observed. Many schools have intersecting hallways, so a teacher or staff member can supervise four
directions by standing at the crossroad. This increases
the safety and security of all students.

Schools can also install video cameras. The criminal
is made to believe that his crime will be videotaped. If
he thinks he is likely to be identified, to be arrested
later, or be unable to escape the property without risk-
ing police capture, he will likely go somewhere else.
School authorities and students can make a difference
when they apply environmental crime-prevention
approaches. Working together, you can create an environment where the criminal feels out of place, insecure,
and out of control. You can create a place where he
thinks he will be seen, identified, and arrested.

The treatment of the location by school authorities,
security personnel, and the police department is called
environmental security. A school planned around ES
(environmental security) principles, incorporates the
CPTED approach. No doubt that some locations are
environmentally designed to decrease crime. Your
school should be constructed with an openness and
clear visibility, which in themselves deter crime. If a
new school is being designed by an architect, have
your parents insist on good surveillance and other
environmental security benefits. Ask your English
teacher to help you write a letter to the school board
based on your fears and your safety concerns.

Avoidance and Deterrence

If you understand how crimes occur and how criminals operate, you will become more aware of local

criminal activity. You will see when a crime is unfolding in front of you. Understanding the elements of crime— the act, the criminal, the victim, and the place—can help you plan a successful *avoidance* and *deterrence* program.

You have several options. First you may choose to report school crime, even if you do it anonymously. This is an important decision. You can also influence your student government. Go into campus politics! Run for office yourself. Even if you don't actively participate in student politics, you can ask your student council to establish rules against weapons, drugs, and gangs.

The principal already enforces some of these rules. The rules are probably published in your Student Handbook, but sometimes student rules and a student-approved Code of Conduct are much more important than the policies administered by adults. So take some responsibility here. Make the decision to take charge and to make a difference.

Students working together can make a big difference. Talk to your principal about security problems at your school. Start a Student Crime-Watch Program. Recruit some of the best students from study hall, pair them up, and let them be hall monitors or serve on a Student Security Patrol. Even fellow students can lower the crime threat at your school.

Maybe your mom and dad are a part of your local Neighborhood Watch program. This is a good plan, and you can use a similar one at your school. Some schools have parent or grandparent volunteer security patrols. If your dad gets off shift work at the right time, he may be able to volunteer for patrols either before, during, or after school. Maybe your mom could accept an assignment as well. Sometimes just the presence of another adult will make all the difference in the world. These adult or peer guardians make a difference. They decrease disruption and crime, and they increase safety and security.

Cooperate with your teachers, counselors, and administrators to create a safer school. Maybe you would like to help design a crime-prevention program unique to your school. Start a student justice system with the approval of school administrators. Publish the new rules. Make sure everyone is properly informed of the new rules, and give at least a week's notice before implementing them. Parents should receive a mailing or hand-delivered notification as well.

Student justice systems help settle disagreements, avoiding confrontations and violence. Just be sure you are consistent and that the rules students agree to are uniformly applied.

Victim Profile

All of us know people who are accident-prone. Thelma Jones has already had three fender benders, and she's only sixteen years old. Keith Addy is always getting hurt doing something idiotic. Last year he broke his front teeth on a telephone pole. Of course, he was reading a science fiction book and walking home at the time.

MAKE A DIFFERENCE

- Start a Student Watch Program!

- Start a Student Justice and Mediation System!

The same concept is evident in crime victimization profiling. Some teenagers are just more crime prone than others. They don't obey the rules of being alert and being aware.

Remember, criminals want an easy target, a "soft target." They look for an opportunity to commit a crime successfully with a vulnerable victim, usually someone who is distracted, isolated, and alone. This is the ideal victim. Remember, most attackers want an ideal victim, not a fight.

The Four Stages of Crime

Every crime has four stages. These stages create the crime development process. The first stage is called *surveillance*. The student criminal watches other students. He is watching to see what he can take, who he can abuse, and who will make a good target.

The surveillance stage may take just a second or two. Sometimes, however, victims are observed over a long period of time. Sometimes the surveillance lasts for weeks or even months, like when a kidnapper

---

VICTIM TRAITS

- Victim is unsure and tentative.
- Victim lacks confidence.
- Victim is easily distracted or is already distracted.
- Victim is easily intimidated.
- Victim is overly trusting.
- Another, but opposing, victim trait is the alert, confident student who is reckless and heedless of risk.

wants to take a child or a rapist wants to attack a particular girl or boy. Sometimes the surveillance is intermittent. The surveillant looks for an opportunity when he or she is not likely to be identified or arrested. He wants to escape with your money or the items he stole from you. He doesn't want to get caught.

Easy escapes are available between the recognition of the surveillance and the start of the invitation. This is the time when you should turn into a local business, cross the street, or step up on the bus as it pauses at the intersection. This is when you should leave.

The second stage is called an *invitation*. The invitation is a distraction. You are walking to school. Someone wants to steal your watch or leather book bag. By engaging you in a conversation, he distracts you and then stops you. When you are stationary, you are a more likely target. Invitations take many forms. Someone may ask you for change or for directions. "Do you know where Mason Street High School is?" If that is where you are going, answer, "Sure, follow me," but whatever you do, don't stop walking. By not stopping, you decrease the likelihood that you will become a crime victim. The person expected you to stop, so you throw his crime plan off track.

The third stage is called a *confrontation*. During the confrontation, the action element of the crime is initiated. First, the criminal asks you for change or for directions in the invitation. You stop, and now he becomes belligerent. "Only a smart-mouthed kid like you would have a nice watch like that; I always wanted one too. Give it to me! Right now."

The fourth stage is the *assault.* The criminal starts pushing you around, punching you, or wrestling your watch away from you. Maybe you can get away. Jerk away and run. Try to escape if you can. The easiest avoidance technique, however, occurred before the assault even started.

It is hard to change the law or the attitude of your attacker. You may have little or no control over the location of an attack, but you can always use victim-avoidance techniques to protect yourself from harm.

Keep your eyes open. Listen! Interpret what you see and hear. If you see a group of gang members or other suspicious persons up ahead, decide what to do before you get too close. Perhaps you should alter your direction. By making the right decision, you, too, can avoid becoming a victim.

THE FOUR STAGES OF CRIME

- Surveillance
- Invitation
- Confrontation
- Assault

chapter 3

Risk Assessment

Jerry is concerned about crime. He is seeing more criminal attack news accounts on TV and is reading more articles in the local paper. More fights have broken out at school this year than ever before. Gang colors are very much in evidence, and drugs were seized by the police last week. Jerry's dad says that "everything must be all right at Lakeland High, or the school authorities would notify us." Mom is not so sure, and she is worried about school safety issues.

Now Jerry wants to know if his school is safe. Is there a security problem at Lakeland? How can he determine the risk factor? He doesn't want his mom to be worried unnecessarily, but he doesn't want to be caught up in violence because he was unaware or wasn't careful. How can he discover whether Lakeland, its grounds, or the walkways going to and from Lakeland High are dangerous?

Determine Your Risk Factor

The FBI, the state police, and your local police units use complex methods to determine crime risk. You don't need to use some intricate logarithm to determine if you are at risk, however. Risk assessments can be completed by those who are conscientiously committed to obtaining good crime information. To make a risk assessment, follow the explanation in the box below.

You need to know your enemy. A risk assessment program can point the way. Knowledge is your first line of defense. Knowledge shows you what to do, where to do it, and how to do it. Obtain the knowledge from your local police precinct, newspapers, radio, or TV broadcasts. Through tabulating summaries of these accounts, you will develop personal and

---

RISK ASSESSMENT

- Collect crime data at your school and in your neighborhood.
- Make a pin map (#1) for all reported crimes. Use colored pins: one color for robbery, another for assault, another for drug sales, etc. Use the pins systematically.
- Make a pin map (#2) for the time periods in which crimes occur. Comparing the reported crime map with the time map will give you perspective and context.
- Make a pin map (#3) showing the age of those arrested or accused.

reliable information on which to base security decisions and with which to determine the risk factor.

Making Risk-Assessment Maps

Three maps and the crime reports of your city for the last year are all you will need. The maps should depict your home or apartment, your school, and at least most of the places you frequent during the course of a particular month.

You will need more than one copy of the map because you need to "show" time, place, and the age of crime victims (and the perpetrators, if known) on your visuals. If the 200 block of Violencia Avenue is a drug sale site, a prostitute hangout, and frequently experiences muggings, street robbery, car hijackings, kidnappings, or rape, you need to know this. You also need to know what time these offenses occur. You can easily misrepresent your risk if you use a fact such as, "there were twenty-two shootings on the 200 block of Violencia Avenue last year; therefore I am at increased risk when I walk down that block." I would avoid the block if I could, just because spinoff problems from site violence occur there sometimes. However, the 200 block may be relatively safe during before-school hours or after-school hours. It may become an urban nightmare around midnight.

Hot Spots

Many schools have crime zones, or "hot spots." Criminologists know that these are the locations where drug pushers, gang members, satanists, and weirdo cults hang out. Sometimes the hot spot is a rest room. When this happens, fearful students often stop using these facilities, but then their physical discomfort decreases their learning ability.

Sometimes the hot spot is a particular hallway or a staircase. Informed students may purposefully avoid these areas until after the bell rings, preferring the criticism of their teacher over an attack or a threat by the school bully, a druggie, or a cult member. If a particular rest room or stairway is the hangout for the "rough crowd," use another rest room or another stairway if possible.

When you attended kindergarten or first grade you were taught to stop, look, and listen before crossing the street. You need to do the same thing to avoid crime. You may believe that the police are supposed to keep you safe. To some extent this belief is accurate, but the officers are usually somewhere else when you need them the most.

As a state police officer, I have investigated over two hundred murders. I never prevented a single killing! I always got there too late. The victim was already dead. Your school security officer will probably be on the other side of the campus when you need him or her the most. Criminals don't normally commit offenses in front of police officers or school administrators. They wait until all adult guardians are out of sight. Since you can't always depend on adults, it becomes your responsibility to avoid crime. "Stop, look, and listen" was good advice when crossing the street. For crime-avoidance purposes, you should continue to watch, look, and listen!

Police officers would call the 200 block of Violencia Avenue a crime "hot spot." Everyone is at increased risk at a crime hot spot. However, if the twenty-two shootings all occurred after midnight and none of the shootings occurred immediately before or after school or during the early evening hours, then the site may not be overly dangerous during daylight hours.

It is really easy for your parents to say, "never walk or drive down the 200 block of Violencia Avenue." This may be good overall advice, but what happens if you live on that block or just one block over? What if you *must* travel through a crime hot spot to get to school every day? What if you *must* walk by gang, drug, mugger, homeless, and prostitute hangouts? A family may be stuck economically and unable to move, or maybe this location is near a parent's work area, so it saves money to be able to walk instead of buying a car or using the city transit service. In this case, the student will need more specific advice.

PINs

A PIN is an imprecise acronym. It stands for Pre-Incident Indicators.[1] Used as a forecasting tool, a PIN can help keep you from harm. A PIN can be based on the actions of others or on a personal observation. Sometimes the PIN comes from a TV, radio, or newspaper report. Some PINs are long range. Some are immediate. Perhaps you have heard that the rival gangs in your school are going to fight next week. This is a strong indicator of impending trouble.

In his book, *Crisis Management: Planning for the Inevitable,* Steven Fink used the words "prodrome," or "prodromal"[2] to describe pre-crisis (or pre-crime) behavior. *Prodrome* is a Greek word meaning "running before." Criminals give us plenty of prodromal indicators. The more you can learn about crime in your neighborhood or at your school, the better off you will be.

Some indicators are immediate, however. Let's say that you are walking to school. Knowledge and awareness of your surroundings are critical to PIN usage, so you should always pay attention to what's going on. You spot three gang members standing across the street. You had an argument with one of them last week. You won the verbal dispute, and some of your friends laughed at him. He was enraged. He shook his finger in your face and screamed, "I'll get even if it's the last thing I ever do." Now you see him pointing at you.

The three gangsters split up. One walks toward you, another runs ahead, and the third guy rushes over to cut you off from behind. This is a prime example of an immediate threat. You should already be reacting, moving, and avoiding the incident. Maybe you should jump into the empty taxi at the curb. Maybe you should step into a local business. Should you fight, they will most definitely beat you into pulp unless you are some special hot shot Karate Kid.

Even if you are the Karate Kid, you'll probably be injured in a three-on-one fight. And even if you win, these guys could come back again—but next time with the whole gang—to begin round two of the fight.

YOUR RISK IS INCREASED WHEN

- gangs operate with impunity.
- illegal drug sales are a "growth" business at your school and community.
- robbers are targeting students at school or near your school.
- rapists are targeting students at your school or near your school.
- MICAs (Mentally Incompetent, Chemically Addicted people) frequent your school area.

Psychologist Gavin DeBecker wrote in *The Gift of Fear: Survival Signals that Protect Us from Violence* that "prediction moves from a science to an art when you realize that preincident indicators are actually part of the incident."[3] There can be many PINs. A threat may be a PIN. In other cases a threat might just be a verbal act, mere rhetoric from a verbally aggressive teenager.

When I was fourteen years old, a bully telephoned. He said, "I'm coming over to your house to beat you up." I waited all afternoon so he'd have his chance. I even cut our grass. Twice I watched him as he rode by on his motorcycle, but he never stopped. His threat was rhetorical. Context is very important in terms of your PIN analysis. In his book, DeBecker wrote: "Context is everything."[4] We must interpret everything we observe or read in context. Seeing with your mind as well as with your eyes provides context.

Fear

DeBecker believes very strongly that fear is an intuition. Why are we afraid on occasion? Why are we comfortable around a tattooed three-hundred-pound biker with earrings but intimidated by an eighty-eight-pound teenager? The intuition of fear is a benefit of life. Don't be ashamed of being afraid. Listen to your fear. Respond to your fear. Use fear as a forecasting tool.

Let's say that your school is dangerous. Gangs, weapons, and student robberies are a part of the daily ritual. Drugs are prevalent. Members of thirteen recognized criminal gangs attend your school. There are nearly twenty-eight hundred students at your school representing some thirteen language groups and the cultures of over forty countries. Police were called in seven times during the last three weeks.

With all of this violence, how can you tell which information is important and which is irrelevant? Students are sometimes numbed by their fear because they are frightened so frequently. When this happens, you often go into denial. You become more at risk because you try to persuade your mind that you shouldn't be scared. You need good and accurate crime information now.

Your risk analysis measurements need to be accurate and precise. You need good information in order to properly assess your school's risk factor and your "personal risk factor." The term *risk assessment* sounds like an imprecise, vague, or scientific term. Fortunately, it's not. The word *risk* applies to all of the possibilities of attack and to all other possible threats.

Receiving and Rating Information

Assessing your risk requires receiving and rating information. There are two different levels of information. One is the eyewitness report. The eyewitness is considered to be a *primary resource.* The witness who overheard someone else's conversation is called a *secondary resource.* Secondary resources are frequently used when gang wars and turf battles are confronted.

As you receive information, you will need to evaluate the source, the information, and the consequences of the information. This evaluation is vital and necessary for any security analysis or risk assessment. Sometimes you may choose to stay silent on a matter, but if you receive information that your friend Johnny is about to be murdered in a gangster initiation, then the consequences of the action require that you at least make an anonymous phone call to report this information. In fact, you should call the police, the principal, and Johnny as well. Wouldn't you want to know if there was a "contract" out on you? You might save Johnny's life. A few weeks from now, he might save yours.

AS YOU RECEIVE INFORMATION

- Evaluate the source
- Evaluate the information
- Evaluate the consequences of the information
- Pray for guidance

A Reliability Index

Once you begin receiving information, you will want to assign a reliability factor to it. Reliable information from a reliable source who has given accurate and dependable information in the past is given a high rating. Information from someone who is not always dependable may be given an unknown rating. Information from someone you do not know at all should be given an even lower rating.

Very reliable information makes sense and can be verified by another quality source of information. Reliable information is consistent with your expectations. It originates with a reliable source and is not in conflict with information you have received from other reliable sources. Suspect information comes either from someone you do not know well or someone you know well enough to question his or her credibility. Suspect information usually cannot be corroborated by any reliable source. If a violent gang is maliciously spreading false rumors (called *misinformation*), you may find that multiple sources of questionable reliability are spreading the same rumor. Question any information that does not fit expectations. Unreliable information, on the other hand, may simply come from a source you do not trust. Unreliable information is usually contradicted by reliable sources and can rarely be verified.

INFORMATION RATING SYSTEM

(1) Very reliable
(2) Reliable
(3) Unknown
(4) Suspect information
(5) Unreliable information

Crime data from your neighborhood indicates what you need to know: where crimes are occurring, when they are occurring, the ages of arrested offenders, or the probable ages of offenders in the cases not solved. It lets you know who the criminals are and how old they are. Now you can plan an informed response. You can act or react appropriately.

What Do the Scriptures Say About Assessing Risk?

I am sure the physician or the psychologist understands better than me as he reads of Jesus healing a diseased body or a diseased mind. I, on the other hand, see and interpret historical attack accounts in a similar manner.

My own life experiences have been in the military, intelligence (gathering and interpreting crime related information), policing, and security professions. So when I read some passages, I see information in terms of my training and experience.

Joseph, the earthly father of Jesus Christ, gave several strong examples of information gathering, intelligence data interpretation, and risk analysis. In just a few short verses you can "see" his actions, as recorded in Matthew. Some of these passages reflect divine intervention. Other passages reflect Joseph's own initiative.

Then being divinely warned in a dream that they should not return to Herod, they (the wise men) departed for their own country another way. Now when they had departed, behold, an angel of the Lord appeared to Joseph in a dream, saying, "Arise, take the young Child and His mother, flee

to Egypt, and stay there until I bring you word;
for Herod will seek the young Child to destroy
Him." When he arose, he took the young Child
and His mother by night and departed for Egypt.
(Matt. 2:12–14)

The wise men who came to worship Jesus were likewise warned and listened to the voice of God. In Matthew 2:11, the wise men worshiped Jesus and presented him with gifts; then they received a message from God. God gave Joseph a message as well.

God told Joseph to flee into Egypt. Joseph traveled initially by night. The Bible does not say whether God told him to do this, yet he did. This was an important security decision. When Joseph returned from Egypt, he likewise gleaned details that greatly increased the safety and security of our Lord Jesus Christ.

Now when Herod was dead, behold, an angel of
the Lord appeared in a dream to Joseph in Egypt,
saying, "Arise, take the young Child and His
mother, and go to the land of Israel, for those who
sought the young child's life are dead." Then he
arose, took the young Child and His mother, and
came into the land of Israel. But when he {Joseph}
heard that Archelaus was reigning over Judea
instead of his father Herod, he was afraid to go
there. And being warned by God in a dream, he
turned aside into the region of Galilee. And he
came and dwelt in a city called Nazareth.
(Matt. 2:19–23)

Joseph was a spiritual man. While he occupied an extraordinary position in history, one with tremendous responsibilities, it seems apparent that those of us who are within the will of the Father will likewise be able to see and know the will of God in adverse times.

chapter 4

Risk Reduction

Vicki lives in the downtown area. Her mom works in a real estate office and is responsible for several hundred apartment rentals. As part of her mom's financial package, they get free rent in a really nice apartment with a doorman. Their apartment building is as safe as any inner-city residence can be, but as soon as Vicki steps away from the protection of her building, she walks into a modern-day horror story.

Vagrants, homeless people, drunks, prostitutes, gang members, and drug pushers frequent the streets between her apartment and the Center for Art, the special high school for talented students that Vicki attends. There are several twenty-four-hour topless bars in the area. Some of Vicki's friends have been harassed by guys who thought they were young prostitutes. Some have even been hugged, pawed, or otherwise embarrassed, and Vicki is scared it will happen to her too. She is very careful about how she dresses and makes sure she always carries her school backpack so everyone will know she is a student. She has taken her name tag off the backpack so strangers won't know her name. Vicki wants to know how to avoid crime. She's asked advice from several of her adult friends, but some of their crime-prevention suggestions conflict.

Put the *U* in Security

For your crime-prevention program to work, you must learn to avoid, or at least reduce the risks to your safety and security. Notice that the word *you* and *your* are used repeatedly. This is because you can't take the *U* out of security! Some cynics might tell you that you can't avoid crime. "If they really want to get you, they'll get you." Often adults, occasionally even a parent, might say "You can't protect yourself against random acts of violence." These are the most frequently repeated myths. Many people accept these myths as some great truth. These myths are usually expressed by people who don't understand crime. I disagree. You *can* learn to be safe.

Security should be a part of your everyday lifestyle. Since the National School Safety Center indicates that most crimes against children and teenagers occur at school, your school is the single most dangerous place you can go, and the incidences of student-on-student and student-on-adult violence have escalated.[1] Of course, a bar or crack house is extremely dangerous, but I am talking about places "normal" kids go.

> Crimes are prevented all the time. It is a myth that you can't do anything about crime. You can!

Do you know what location is the next most dangerous? No, it is not the entertainment center, the movie theater, the bowling alley, the skating rink, or the local hangout. The next most dangerous place is your home. This is where you probably feel most safe and secure, unless you live in an abusive home. This is where you let your guard down and don't have to live by all these security rules. Right? Wrong! Security must become a part of your lifestyle at home, in the community, and at school.

MANAGING CRIME RISKS

- Remove some risks
- Reduce some risks
- Spread some risks
- Transfer some risks
- Accept risk

Risks Can Be Managed

You may not be able to eliminate risk in your life, but you can influence it. One thing you cannot afford to do, though, is to ignore risk. Risks can be managed—through *risk removal, risk reduction, risk spreading,* and *risk transference.* One of the first murders I was associated with as a young police investigator involved the killing of a sixteen-year-old girl. Tragically, she was in the wrong place at the wrong time. Her parents had told her that she could not visit a particular night spot featuring live entertainment, dancing, and beer. She and her boyfriend wanted to hear the new band, so they disobeyed. They just bought a soft drink and were having a good time—until a gunfight broke out between a man, his wife, and her boyfriend. The boyfriend missed his self-defense shot but drilled the sixteen-year-old dead-center. She was dead before she hit the floor. The cause of death was a gunshot wound, but the reason for her death was that she didn't obey her parents.

OBEY YOUR PARENTS!

Children, obey your parents in the Lord, for this is right. "Honor your father and mother," which is the first commandment with promise: "That it may be well with you and you may live long on the earth." (Eph. 6:1–3)

Everyone manages risk to some degree. Your parents have checking accounts and keep extra money in a savings account that is federally insured, protecting their money against robbery, fraud, or bank failure. These accounts are much safer than keeping the money at your home where you may be burgled, robbed, or victimized by fire. When your mom shops for Christmas, she probably puts expensive packages in the trunk rather than inside the car, as she continues shopping. This decreases the likelihood of a car burglary because the thief doesn't know if there are valuables there or not. He wants a sure thing! If she put the package on the backseat, she might lose a window as well as the package when the thief attacks.

Risk removal for a teenager could involve leaving an expensive watch at home. If your dad's expensive notebook computer is likely to be taken, you should leave it at home. If you have an expensive jacket, wear an inexpensive one to school. Risk removal can save your life.

If you have one hundred dollars, *risk reduction* means you should take only enough cash for your daily needs. Leave the rest at home or, even better, in your bank account. Risk reduction significantly influences whether you will be selected for a crime. Reducing the amount of money you take to school each day helps protect you from harm.

Risk spreading also lowers your risk. Let's say you are going to the bank after school today. You have one hundred dollars in cash. You put twenty-five dollars in each of your four trouser pockets. Robbers usually reach for the wallet. They may get the wallet and the twenty-five dollars in it, but they won't get all your cash because they won't look in the other pockets. This is a good example of risk spreading.

Risk transference is another technique for lowering your risk. One example of this technique is the purchase of an insurance policy. Another is the transfer of a store's money in an armored car, moving the loss risk to the armored car company instead of the store. A good example of personal risk transference could occur between family members. Little Bobby has had his lunch money stolen twice, so big brother carries the cash and gives it to the teacher. The larger brother accepts the financial risk.

> Reducing the amount of cash you take to school each day lowers the possibility that you will be a crime victim.

Another way transference works is when a bully or a thief is transferred from a regular school to an alternative school. Gang members are redistributed among several other schools. So instead of having twelve members of the "Bumblebee Mafia" at one school, there are only two members at six different schools. Sometimes this doesn't work out because these gangsters recruit new members at the other schools. Maybe some of these kids will have to be sentenced to the state youth prison for some attitude adjustment. This is a "real" transfer.

All crime cannot be removed, reduced, spread, or transferred. Some crime risks just have to be accepted. Banks may be robbed, but very few close their doors because of robbery. Convenience stores and liquor stores have a very high risk factor, but you find them in almost every part of town. Many stores are open twenty-four hours a day. This increases their risk.

All risk can never be eliminated. So you do the best you can, but you do your best conscientiously. You practice the principles of crime deterrence, crime avoidance, and crime prevention.

Are You A Target?

There are several crime-deterrence and crime-prevention terms you should understand. The first term is *soft target*. A soft target is an easy target. The next term you should remember is *target hardening*. Target hardening makes it much more difficult for someone to commit a crime and increases the risk for the criminal. He or she is much more likely to be seen, identified, and arrested for committing the crime. When Nehemiah "set a watch

against them (their enemies)" (Neh. 4:9) over the walls of
Jerusalem, he hardened his target and made it more difficult for a successful attack. Let's look carefully at the concept of a soft and hard target.

A Soft Target

Suzy brought eighty-five dollars to school today.
She is excited about clothes shopping with her mom
this afternoon, so she tells all her friends. The money
is in her purse. She has her lunch money in her pocket,
as is appropriate. During lunch, however, she leaves
her purse inside her homeroom.

Suzy and her eighty-five dollars are a soft target. It
will be an easy crime. Johnny is an experienced and
successful thief; he's been stealing since he was four
years old. He isn't bright enough to finish his algebra
homework, but he knows how to add Suzy's eighty-
five dollars to his bankroll. Hearing her discussion, he
eats quickly and sneaks back to the homeroom when
no one is there. As surreptitiously as a cat burglar, he
steals Suzy's bankroll.

Moving quickly to the rest room, he hides the
money (four twenties and one five) inside his socks. He
figures that even if he should become a suspect, the
principal will just search his pockets and book bag. He
knows school administrators can get in trouble when
they strip-search a minor, and it would take a strip
search to find the eighty-five dollars. Johnny doesn't
need to worry, however. Suzy won't even realize she has
been victimized until she is ready to pay for the really
nice outfit she and her mom find at the mall.

A Hard Target

Jimmy Smith's dad just bought an exceptionally expensive notebook computer. Mr. Smith is an engineer and runs all sorts of complex mathematical equations through his notebook. The computer cost $8300, and the math/science/engineering software cost another $3600. He has nearly $12,000 invested in the new notebook and its programs.

Mr. Overby, Jimmy's Calculus II teacher, upon learning of this exceptional computer, asked Jimmy to bring the computer to school for a demonstration. Mr. Overby called Jimmy's dad and carefully worked out secure arrangements for this valuable piece of property.

First, Jimmy rides to school with his mom instead of riding the bus. The computer notebook is in his backpack along with his books. The demonstration has not been previously announced, so it is a surprise. Mr. Overby is waiting for Jimmy at the school entrance. As Jimmy exits from the car, the calculus teacher takes the computer to the teachers' lounge and secures the notebook in his personal locker with a quality padlock. The teachers' lounge can be entered only through the reception area of the principal's office; students don't have access.

This is a good example of target hardening. First, those involved planned for a risk. In fact, Jimmy's dad had already purchased computer insurance, so even if the computer was stolen or destroyed, he would not lose all of his financial investment. The second security measure was to ensure that the computer was promptly taken by Mr. Overby, a teacher and a responsible adult. It is no longer in Jimmy's care. Third, the computer notebook was placed in a secured locker in the teachers' lounge. Only teachers can enter, and Mr. Overby protects his locker with a quality lock. Jimmy's dad plans to come by the school on his way home from work, and Mr. Overby will personally return the computer. Jimmy will go home on the bus, but without the computer.

Could someone steal the notebook? Of course, but it would be very difficult, and there would be a very high risk. There was very little risk, however, on the eighty-five-dollar theft by Johnny. He just walked into an empty classroom and took what he wanted.

Jimmy Smith, his dad, and Mr. Overby planned to minimize their risk. Their preparation increased the security for the computer notebook. Suzy didn't make any arrangements at all. Then she bragged about the shopping trip to all of her friends. Suzy never had anything stolen from her, so she believed that every-one in her class was just as honest as she. Because she was so trusting, she didn't realize that her money was gone until she tried on a darling outfit that fit per-fectly. She couldn't buy it. In fact, she left the store in tears.

Taking money to school, especially larger sums, is always risky. However, Suzy could have lowered her risk by remaining silent about the money and not mentioning the shopping trip. She also could have put the money in a small wallet or money clip in the front pocket of her jeans. She could have told her friends about the shopping trip the next day, as she showed off her new clothes. At the very least, she should have taken her purse with her wherever she went. Probably the best option would have been for her mother to hold the eighty-five dollars in safekeeping. Each of these steps would have increased Suzy's personal security and protected the eighty-five dollars from theft. Each of these actions are good examples of target hardening.

Friendliness

Students who are friendly are less likely to be attacked by a young criminal. Look at other students. Smile at them and greet them as a friend. "Hi, how are you today?" This simple statement is friendly, but it is also a crime prevention advantage. Furthermore, it is scriptural: "And be kind to one another, tenderhearted, forgiving one another" (Eph. 4:32). During the attack at Littleton High School, some students were targeted; others weren't. Seventeen-year-old Brooks Brown's life was spared even though he was one of the first students to be confronted by the killers. When he came face-to-face with Eric Harris, the shooter instructed, "Brooks, I like you, now get out of here. Go home!" Being friendly to others, especially "outsiders" can save your life.

Look at people when you greet them. Make brief eye contact and nod at them. However, don't maintain eye contact. Some gang members might interpret this as an insolent nonverbal challenge. A stare could be easily misunderstood. Many gangs use a stare to intimidate others. A stare is especially inappropriate for girls because a

> Students who are friendly are less likely to be attacked by criminals.

creepy guy may think you are interested in him. However, a brief look, a smile, and a nod is a crime deterrent. You are being polite, but you are also indicating that you noticed that person. Psychologists tell us that these are subliminal messages. The look communicates: "I noticed you and I can identify you in a police lineup." Identifying *who* is the most important part of your crime-prevention quest. Keep your eyes on the who. No one was ever attacked, robbed, or raped by a what, when, where, why, or how. Nice people don't think that way, but delinquents do. A non-threatening subliminal message can even save your life.

If the guy Cindy just looked at and said hi to was planning to steal her purse, he probably just changed his mind. Why? Because Cindy can place him at the crime scene during the time period when the theft occurred. This is dangerous for him. It is a significant risk. Even though he wants her money, he does not want to be labeled as a thief. He doesn't want to be suspected either. He's not a strong-armed rob-

> Look but don't stare at those around you.

ber; he wants to remain anonymous. Last, but not least, he doesn't want to be caught. He doesn't want to be arrested. He wants to be trusted so he feels comfortable to steal again in the same room. Since Cindy saw him and can place him at the scene, he probably will not steal today.

You can make a difference at school. Crime rates can be influenced positively anywhere. Crimes can't be influenced when you do not help deter or prevent them. Never let your guard down. In dangerous schools everyone should implement good security practices. Vigilance should be the first approach.

The Bible and Crime Prevention

Many crime problems were confronted in the Scriptures. In the fourth chapter of Nehemiah, the people of Judah were rebuilding first the wall and then the city of Jerusalem. These Hebrew people were "of the remnant left behind." The Book of Nehemiah is a historical account of the rebuilding and the difficulties the Hebrews experienced during this period. Nehemiah was very security conscious. Nehemiah 1:11 reveals that Nehemiah was the king's cupbearer.

Cupbearer is an interesting term, one that doesn't relate to most current positions. Was Nehemiah a waiter, a lowly servant in the House of Artaxerxes? I think not. Historically, a cupbearer was a member of the king's security detail. Today the cupbearer in the United States would be a member of the Secret Service assigned to the president's security detail.

Nehemiah tasted the king's foods and beverages to ensure their quality but also to make sure that they were not spoiled or poisoned. The cupbearer was required to consume each food and drink product served at any of the king's meals. If the cupbearer wasn't careful, then he, too, could die. This practice insured the security of the king's meals.

Evidently, Nehemiah earned the king's respect, so Artaxerxes allowed him to return to Jerusalem. The king even bankrolled the Temple reconstruction budget.

When Nehemiah traveled to Jerusalem, he gave the king's letters of introduction and safe passage to the local leaders. Initially Nehemiah kept the wall reconstruction plan a secret. This, too, was part of his security plan. There was no need for the enemies of Jerusalem to be forewarned or to prepare early counteroffensives. Sanballat, Tobiah, the Ammonites, and the Ashdodites were angered over the rebuilding, and conspired together to fight against the builders, hindering the defensive wall reconstruction project (Neh. 4:7–8).

It is very important to know what Nehemiah and the workers did at that time, and the order in which they did it. First they prayed! (Neh. 4:9). Then they "set a watch against them day and night" (Neh. 4:9).

At times the work was difficult. On occasion, only one-half of the workers were rebuilding the wall. The others were fully armed and armored, waiting for the inevitable attacks of their enemies. While schools are not at war, and you are not to use weapons like guns, knives, and spears, nonetheless, "putting up a watch" and being observant and aware is an early step in crime prevention, avoidance, and deterrence.

Nehemiah dealt appropriately with the problem confronting Jerusalem. Likewise, you can deal successfully with crime at your own school. Develop an avoidance and deterrence plan that would be acceptable to God.

Let's say that a bully named Billy abuses young kids, intimidates teenagers, and frequently throws "fits." When he gets mad, he fights just about anybody who is around. Billy's crimes are visible to all.

NEHEMIAH DEVELOPED A SECURITY PLAN!

- First and foremost, he prayed.
- Then he "set up a watch" to ensure that his workers would not be caught unaware by raiders.

Lots of kids are so afraid of Billy that they keep silent about his crimes, privately hoping he won't bother them.

Billy's crimes remain secret because the kids are so afraid of him that they won't report him to the principal or the police. The secrecy allows Billy to maintain power. What could you do to solve this security dilemma without having to confront Billy?

In some cities, solving this dilemma is relatively easy. Let's say that Billy carries a switchblade knife or a pistol to school. He uses the weapon to threaten young kids and other teenagers. A switchblade knife is illegal in any state, but any knife is illegal at school. Most schools have an expulsion policy: Bring a gun or knife to school and you are expelled for a year. You are arrested and prosecuted before the juvenile court as well. This would be the way to remove Billy. The next time you know he has the knife, call the principal's office *anonymously* if you are afraid to make a personal complaint.

Some cities have Crime Stopper programs. Memphis, Tennessee, and Albuquerque, New Mexico, run school Weapons Watch programs under their Crime Stopper programs. Students who legitimately report weapons at school are awarded fifty dollars anonymously. Wouldn't this be wonderful? You get rid of the gun, you get rid of Billy, and you get the reward money as well. Actually, you get a double award—the money and his dismissal from school.

Perhaps you should call the police. In the state of Washington, you can call 1-800-862-GUNS (all calls are confidential). After installing this toll-free hotline, authorities quickly reported an average of 187 calls each school day. These calls came from all over the state and included large, small, city, suburban, and rural schools. When an anonymous phone call comes in to the Washington State GUNS hotline, police authorities respond immediately.

The police will probably bring a dog capable of smelling guns and drugs. They will check Billy's book bag and his locker and let the dog screen the area. If Billy is using a weapon or drugs, he goes to jail and doesn't come back to your school. He doesn't even get to know who "informed." Billy is removed as a threat, possibly never to return again. He will be transferred to an alternative school for delinquents. He won't even get to be a bully at the alternative school because there is usually one teacher for each five or six students.

Knowledge is power. Use your knowledge for your own safety and the safety of your friends. Students often become so accustomed to their school security technology that they forget the fact that closed circuit television units were installed at their school. At one school, students who were being "extorted" (their lunch money was being taken) arranged to stand in front of the school camera when "their" thief arm-twisted, socked, and stole. It appeared accidental, but it wasn't. It was a setup, carefully arranged by his victims.

Contrary to what you may think, this arrangement is not a crime known as entrapment. You are just arranging for a thief and bully to steal from you in front of the camera—and not down the hall or on the school yard. The principal comes out and catches Billy. It looks like it was coincidental, but it wasn't. Set up your bully! Think how pleasant that experience would be. Maybe your bully will play a role on "World's Dumbest Criminals."

chapter 5

Your Personal Security Program

Rhonnie lives in a neighborhood about three blocks from her school. Jenny lives near her, and they usually walk to school and church together. In years past, neither of the girls felt uncomfortable walking to school, but things seem different this year. The quickest route to school takes them right past some gangster-looking guys. Rhonnie doesn't like the way they stare, and she thinks they are mumbling inappropriate remarks; but she can't hear them clearly, so she isn't sure.

Rhonnie is apprehensive, however. Chill bumps went down her spine the last time she and Jenny came in contact with the gangsters. Rhonnie wants to use another route, so they don't have to pass these creeps every day. Jenny disagrees. "The way we are going is the most direct route, and we know those guys from school," she says. "Everything will be all right! Don't worry." Their argument is intense, so both girls choose individual routes the next day. Each girl walks alone.

Rhonnie walks to school without incident, but

Jenny is crying when they meet for first period. The gangster-guys had surrounded Jenny when she was alone, making inappropriate remarks. They asked her if she was a virgin and wanted to know if she would date their leader. They crudely and vividly described how Jenny's jeans fit and how snug her sweater was. A Christian, her dress habits are very modest, but Jenny felt cheap after they had talked about her body. After Jenny ran away, she became frightened about what could have happened that morning and what might happen in the future. Rhonnie and Jenny always walk the alternate route together now, and they have had no further incidents.

Sara lives in a small farm community. Everybody knows everybody for miles around. She and her parents have always felt safe and secure there. Sara walks nearly three miles to school every day. She is alone for over half of her walk. The other day, on a lonely stretch, a stranger pulled up beside her and asked for directions. He said he had a map and asked her to show him the way to a local farm. She wanted to help, so she walked over to his car. When she looked in, however, she didn't see a map at all. All she could see was that this guy was naked from the waist down. Sara screamed and ran home. Her folks were glad that the pervert didn't grab her while she was most vulnerable (when she was really close to his car). Sara knows that she will never walk up to a stranger's car door again.

Be Careful

If you were on tour in an African jungle or a Latin American swamp, you probably would be very careful about stepping on snakes or into quicksand. We are afraid of things we don't know much about. As tourists we might not have the skills necessary to avoid either of these risks. However, right here at home, we often deny our risks. We have gotten so used to our risks that we do not even consciously consider them anymore.

How many teens step off the curb quickly when the traffic light changes in their favor? Yet, is it not also possible that the approaching driver has defective brakes, is inattentive, or drunk? Is it not possible that by stepping out without looking both ways, you increase the likelihood of a collision or a hit-and-run? Many young people step right out into high crime-rate districts just as casually. They walk into big-time trouble without ever seeing it in advance. You need to be able to see if you are going to avoid trouble, if you are going to be secure.

Never Delegate Your Security

Delegation means to appoint or assign someone else to represent you. Sometimes we do this politically, but it is a very poor idea in terms of personal protection. It is very easy to say, "I don't have to worry about crime. That's why we have policemen. It is *their* job to protect me." With an attitude like this, you can rest assured that you will become one of every four citizens who are victimized by a serious crime within the next four years.

I was a police officer and later served as a criminal investigator. I never investigated a rape, murder, robbery, or an arson that hadn't already happened. People who depended on me to prevent their crime or to protect them from crime were tragically disappointed. I did all I could, but I never prevented even one of these crimes.

It is unreasonable for you to believe that officers will be there to protect you when you need them. It is a *myth* to believe that you can always depend on the police or anyone else. A police officer won't be there when you are frightened. He probably won't be close enough to hear you scream. It is *your* responsibility to avoid crime, to deter crime, and to prevent crime.

Personal Security

Personal security is the simple act of accepting responsibility for your own safety. You accept this responsibility just as you accept other responsibilities. The *total* responsibility for your own safety is yours. Governments and institutions can and should take steps to deter crime, but since they err so much, you won't be able to depend on any person but yourself.

Everyone has a personal security program. Locking your house or car is a good example. Locking your clothes, watch, and money in a safe place while you are at the gymnasium is another example. At home, a barking dog is also a good crime deterrent. Likewise, you can do many things before school, on the way to school, at school, and on the way home to increase your safety and decrease your risk.

> A personal security program is the simple act of protecting yourself from physical harm.

Your security program is a "target-hardening approach." Remember, a hard target is a difficult target.

An easy target, or victim, is a soft one. Teenagers who become target-hardened are much less likely to be victimized. In its most ideal form, a target-hardened individual is simply overlooked. It is as if the crook never even sees this person as a target. They see someone else instead.

In addition to a security plan, you also need to develop two personal behavioral characteristics into high-level skills: *observation* and *mental alertness.* "Everybody sees," you say. "Everybody observes!" Yes and no.

Be Alert

The truly observant person is mentally alert. He or she is aware of unsafe areas and that some relatively safe locations are dangerous at specific times. The very best crime-avoidance strategy is to be aware. A perfectly safe location at 8:00 AM may be incredibly dangerous at midnight. Observant students always examine and interpret their surroundings. They look, see, interpret, and detect, and thus avoid problems for themselves and others. They create the impression of self-confidence and self-control. They trust their instincts because their instincts are finely tuned.

They look—*really look*—as they walk down school hallways or as they sit down at lunch. As you walk school hallways, you need to look at each student you pass. Try to gain just a moment of eye contact with each one, but don't stare. Staring is considered an aggressive behavior. Guys fight other guys over stare games. Just glance at other students when you walk by. When possible, say hi. Be friendly. The eye contact should not be intimidating or challenging. Staring will raise your crime risk if the viewer thinks you are challenging him.

You accomplish something every time you look at a passerby and greet that person. You send a message. The message is basically this: "I saw you. I recognize you. I can identify you." This is a powerful restraint on the part of the individual offender, especially at a public school. Predators tend to avoid those who look like they may respond assertively. They want meek and quiet victims, not someone who will yell or fight, so they pick on people who look down, listen to headsets, and don't pay attention. If you have the tendency to stare down at the floor when you feel bad or are depressed, work on remedying this habit. You'll be safer when you stop.

In many cases, victims attract the attention of predators because of the way they walk, talk, or dress. The student who is afraid, walking with his head down, is an inviting target. Students who send a message that they are shy, unsure, uncoordinated, or lack confidence reassure the criminal. While wealth and really nice clothes, jewelry, or watches increase the likelihood of being targeted, criminals do not always choose the affluent; they choose the easy victim. They choose the first suitable victim available.

What Do the Scriptures Say?

The Scriptures give us guidance on how we should act. In Titus, Paul recommended that the young women be "discreet, chaste" (Titus 2:4). The young men were also instructed to be "sober-minded" (Titus 2:6). All Christians were exhorted to, "in all things showing yourself to be a pattern of good works; in doctrine showing integrity, reverence, incorruptibility, sound speech that cannot be condemned, that one who is an opponent contrary may be ashamed, having nothing to say of you" (Titus 2:7–8).

Be friendly to all. This is not the superficial friendliness of somebody running for student council office. It is the consistent friendliness that all of us who love the Lord should be able to express to the world. Friendliness has many advantages, not only for witnessing, but also for safety.

Friendly students are less likely to be molested. Bullies and the gangs usually bother students they don't like or respect. If you are popular and well-liked, you are less likely to be attacked. Loners and students who are disliked are at higher risk.

Vigilance

Observation skill and pre-criminal activity interpretation are necessary in any security plan. Vigilance is another necessity. *Vigilance* simply means to stay alert or awake and be watchful for trouble. In truly dangerous schools, you must always be vigilant, even in the classroom; but your primary threats are in the hallways, the cafeteria, the gymnasium, and the school yard. More school murders and the more serious assaults occur in the lunchroom than at any other school location.

Vigilant students never let anyone get close enough to them to compromise their activities. They do not walk alone or unescorted through dangerous areas or in any areas unsupervised by guardians. Robberies, assaults, and rapes increase when potential victims are inattentive and careless. Vigilance and care lower your risk considerably.

Vigilance is also scriptural. Look up the seventh chapter of Judges. God told Gideon to lead an army. Gideon recruited an army of thirty-two thousand. God wanted to show that the Israelites would win the battle by his might alone, so he wanted fewer men. Twenty-two thousand men went home; ten thousand remained. The final test for the three hundred men who won the Battle of Midian was one of vigilance. The observant men reached their hands down into the brook and lapped the water from their hands while looking about for their enemies. These men would not be caught unaware, even in a crowd. The careful, wary men were used by God; the rest were sent home.

Crime avoidance should become a way of life. It is based on certain skills, the most important of which is continual observation and awareness. Be wary! Always watch for danger! Keep up with the crime trends in your neighborhood. When you know how the crime occurs, when it occurs, and why it occurs, you have several more weapons available in your crime-avoidance toolkit.

TARGET HARDENING

- Learn about crime in your area.
- Be vigilant.
- Observe your environment at all times. Look for threats continuously.
- React immediately. Don't even think about it. If you see a threat or a risk, do what the military does. Take countermeasures immediately.

chapter 6

Everyday Security Decisions

Jody and her brother Jim attend Bigsville High. The school is named appropriately because it is one huge complex with an elementary, middle, and high school. Thirty-eight hundred students ranging from age five to eighteen arrive on this campus five days a week, nine months a year. The school board thought that neighborhood schools were too expensive and it was more efficient to bring everyone together in one central complex. Though each school has a separate building, every student must come together in the same traffic pick-up lines, parking lots, bus zone, and cafeteria.

The school has grown by leaps and bounds as more and more new students have transferred in. The cozy little-town atmosphere is now lost at Bigsville High, which is just a human warehouse for kids—lots of them. The school board thinks that big classes are OK too. "It saves money," the members say.

Jody and Jim are stuck in an impersonal environment—a school too big. The teachers are so stressed out and tired that they spend all of their time working with either the very best or the very worst students. The guys and gals in the middle must succeed or fail on their own. Lots of students are angry, rebellious, and hostile. They aren't getting a good education, and they know it. Their futures are at stake because only the best students will pass the college entrance exams. There are no gangs here, and the school is relatively drug free. There are just too many people and too many tensions. Fights break out frequently.

How do Jody and Jim plan for their safety? What decisions must they make each day to stay safe at school? Deciding what they wear, what they take with them or leave behind, and how they are going to act are all very important.

Deciding What to Wear

Clothing that reflects you and your personality can be distinctive. When you dress in *your* colors and *your* styles, you look good and feel better about yourself. The cost of your clothes, however, influences crime prevention. You should never wear "too much" wealth.

Picture this scenario. Jack is wearing $200 Nikes, $135 designer jeans, a $78 shirt, and a $385 Starter jacket. He has an $850 sports watch, a $900 gold chain around his neck, and a $500 gold-braid wristlet.

Louise is wearing an ensemble that cost $375 and a leather-sleeved Starter jacket costing $345. Her watch, earrings, bracelet, anklet, and necklace are valued at over $1,500. Dominic is wearing high-priced clothes, including a full-length leather coat, valued at $750 and a $1,100 gold necklace.

Each of these young people is at high risk! In other words, Jack, Louise, and Dominic have a much higher likelihood of being robbed than any of their friends. Louise is also more likely to be raped. Once she has been cut off and isolated for the robbery, the offender may decide to take more than her valuables. Always remember that your clothing may be the first attraction that singles you out as a criminal target.

Remember Joseph!

Read the historical account of a father who had a favorite son. This event is recorded in the Bible in Genesis 37. Jacob had many sons but was partial to the son of his favorite wife. When Joseph was seventeen, he was given a tunic (jacket) of many colors. This clothing was far better than any Jacob had given his other sons. Joseph had some weaknesses too. He was a tattletale and had gotten his brothers in trouble, and he also bragged about dreams in which he was the master of the family.

The coat was a symbol of wealth and of favored-son status. The brothers coveted their father's love, and they were jealous of Joseph because of the jacket and his preferred status. They felt just like you would feel if your parents gave your brother a high-priced new outfit and went to an inexpensive second-hand store for yours. Some of the brothers wanted to kill Joseph, but they sold him into slavery instead.

Whenever you wear clothing that attracts the eye of your peers, you also attract the eye of criminals and delinquents. Designer jeans, Starter jackets, leather apparel, and expensive sports shoes decrease your level of safety in today's world. The clothing is like a crime magnet. It was true in Genesis 37:18–24, and it is true today.

My own five children wore clothing purchased at the local Wal-Mart or Big K. If we lived in other parts of the United States, we would have picked some other value stores to shop in. Our children were safer this way, even if we really didn't have any other choice.

School Uniforms?

Many schools now require school uniforms. School uniforms provide many advantages for students: they eliminate the economic class distinctions of the poorer versus the wealthier students; they reduce the stigma of wealth; they eliminate some of the gang colors ever-present in many schools; they lower the likelihood of a sneak thief targeting your locker or gym basket (Who would want to steal a school uniform?); and, they lower the risk of criminal attack in any form by any other student at that school.

If your school does not have uniforms, you should dress comfortably but inexpensively. I know that designer jeans are preferred, but discount clothing stores sell clothing that will fit well. Furthermore, you can find colors and styles for shirts, jeans, blouses, and dresses that will reflect favorably upon your personality. Be careful when selecting clothing! This is one time you need to think like a thief, a crook, or a rapist. If you pick red, black, or some other vivid color, will you be at more risk?

Teenagers wearing bright clothing are easily noticed. Girls wearing skintight clothes or microminis are always spotted. In fact, in a crowd, they are noticed first. You don't want to be the first one noticed by a criminal or a juvenile delinquent. Don't let a crook's eye stop on you. Dress in the same colors as everyone else, and you won't stand out. What you wear and carry with you can identify you as an easy target. It can also signal that you are a more difficult target.

What you wear and what you carry can also make it easier to fend off an attacker or to escape. Dress more for defense than for looks. You can run faster in tennis shoes than in loafers, boots, or heels. Also loose-fitting slacks are better for running or self-defense.

Don't Let His Eye Stop on You

Test the concept "Don't let a crook's eyes stop on you." Go up to the second or third floor of a school or downtown building. Look out a window facing the sidewalk. Watch the people walking by. Who do you look at first? Who do you look at twice? Who do you look at longer? Why did these particular people attract your attention? The reason requires some speculation, but it also requires careful analysis.

In this exercise, think like a thief, a robber, or even a rapist. Quite often the eye stops on someone who dresses differently or wears bright colors or unique styles of clothing. Sometimes a behavioral characteristic or peculiarity is what stops the criminal eye. The safest person on the street is someone who looks like most others of his or her age or sex. The person who stands out because of clothing is more likely to be victimized. Anonymity is an advantage in this respect.

- The safest person on the street is someone who looks and dresses like everyone else.
- The person with the highest risk is dressed uniquely or carries obvious wealth.
- Anonymity is an advantage as a crime-prevention tactic.

This same philosophy should reflect your posture and the way you walk. Timid, shy people are much more likely to become crime victims. The young person who walks erectly, pulls his or her shoulders back, and watches the environment is less likely to become a victim! The person who has poor posture, looks down as he or she walks, and does not observe the surroundings makes an excellent victim and is much more likely to be attacked.

Size, weight, and age may be important factors when crooks select their next target, but these factors are much less important than most students believe. A feisty seven-year-old girl may project the image that she will not be a good target, while the "head-in-the-clouds" nineteen-year-old mushbrain sends out the message that he will be a great target.

Girls, remember that criminals make their decisions to attack based on sight and intuition. They attack on reflex, like a fish snapping at a minnow. If you are walking to a friend's apartment dressed in shorts, a miniskirt, and a tank top, or a skin tight exercise suit, you can be assured that many eyes are stopping on you, appraising you. The eye stops on bright clothes, tight-fitting clothes, and immodest hemlines or bustlines. Most of these appraisals are innocent.

Guys are finding you attractive, and other girls are wishing they were as pretty as you. Some of these observers, however, may be criminals. Moreover, some of these viewers may even be rapists. Don't dress so extravagantly or immodestly that the eye always stops on you. It just isn't safe, for boys or girls!

A Scripturally Based Dress Code for Girls and Women

Women of the Middle East were very modest in their dress code. In fact, many still are, except for those who have adapted western dress standards. While these standards may sound like they are nearly two thousand years old (and they are), they are still current and appropriate for today's young women. Women who dress modestly are safer and more secure in dangerous environments. Here is what the disciple Peter told Christian women and girls in the early church:

> *Do not let your adornment be merely outward— arranging the hair, wearing gold, or putting on fine apparel—rather let it be . . . the hidden beauty of a gentle and quiet spirit, which is very precious in the sight of God. For in this manner, in former times, the holy women who trusted in God also adorned themselves.* (1 Pet. 3:1–5)

Knowing How to Walk

The way you dress is not the only crime victimization problem. The way you walk is important too. You want to send a nonverbal message to anyone watching, a positive message that communicates that you will not be a good crime victim! A negative or passive message sends a signal that you will be a good victim, so watch your environment, pull your shoulders back, and walk with an obvious purpose. It is an assertive posture and a healthy one. Girls should not affect a woman's walk. High heels accentuate an ultrafeminine walk, but a sensual stroll is dangerous. Don't display your figure by a pronounced walk. Guys will notice you without these obvious affectations.

To send the subliminal message, "I will not be an easy crime victim," you need to walk erect and with confidence. You also need to walk in the safest locations. If there are no students in the hallway, the safest route is in the center of the hall. Then if someone initiates a confrontation, you can move in more directions. You are not likely to be pinned against the wall unless you were not being observant.

If it is class-change time, your safest location is to the right, adjacent to the wall. You are more vulnerable when students are both to your right and to your left. You are also more vulnerable if you are adjacent to students moving in the opposite direction. You are *less* vulnerable when all the students adjacent to your space are moving in the same direction.

Deciding What You Take with You and What You Leave Behind

Clothing is a strong component in anyone's crime-prevention arsenal. The right clothes decrease your victimization probability. The wrong clothes increase the likelihood of being targeted by a criminal. This isn't all, however. Many possessions also increase your likelihood of being targeted. One is a Walkman-type radio or disc player. Anyone listening to a radio program, music, or a portable CD player has significantly restricted his or her hearing. The person can't hear the street gang approaching from behind or the out-of-control vehicle. Thus, music lovers become crime or accident statistics, and you hear about these folks on the evening news and read about them in the newspapers.

You should not take anything to school that you do not need. If art class is only on Friday afternoons, you do not need to take the art book with you every day unless you plan a special review during study hall. Every book's weight decreases your ability to flee and to react. Leaving the extra books behind also minimizes your loss should you be targeted by a thief.

Most of the junk in your book bag, attaché, or purse could be left at home. Take what you need, but leave the rest behind. Sometimes you take things that increase your risk and the likelihood you will be targeted by a criminal.

Let's say you are going to a math class. Your dad's calculator may increase the likelihood that you will be victimized, especially if only two or three calculators are available in the room. If everyone has a simple, inexpensive, basic calculator, your multifunctional trigonometric, calculus, and engineering model may be the best and most expensive in the room or even in the entire school. By carrying the fancy model, you significantly increase the likelihood that you will be targeted.

The same thing is true of computer notebooks and electronic record-keeping aids. They are nice, but since these same items are frequently stolen at your dad or and mom's workplace, they will certainly be tempting in a school environment.

Girls, take a good look at your purse. Do you really need all that junk? When was the last time you used that purple-tinted, sequined lip ice? Do you always put your money in your purse, or could you use a wallet like the guys do? You could put your money in your pocket. If somebody wants the wallet badly enough, just throw it down and run. The robber probably wants the money first.

Since you plan to throw the wallet, you shouldn't leave anything in it that you can't lose. This also applies in a purse snatching. If somebody grabs your purse and runs, you won't lose everything because you've already transferred your cash to a wallet. Buy a small, inexpensive cloth wallet that doesn't protrude like a leather, folding one does. It won't show or be noticeable. Since the wallet is in your pocket, you won't lose too much if your purse is snatched. You've already curtailed your loss by spreading your risk and by living a crime-avoidance lifestyle.

- Carry your purse closed.
- Secure your purse with a strap.
- Keep your money in your pocket.
- Keep your car keys in your pocket.
- Keep your house keys in your pocket.
- If somebody grabs your purse, let him have it. Then run and yell!

Street-Crime Alarms

Several types of street robbery alarms are available, or you can purchase a police whistle. These noisemakers are excellent defensive weapons. Personal alarms and whistles are most effective in crowds. You can even put one in your purse or attaché and loop the pull chord over your wrist. Then if someone snatches your bag, the security chord is separated from the alarm. Some of these make a tremendous noise. One really expensive one (it costs more than three thousand dollars) has a mild electrical charge. A thief steals your dad's security attaché and hears an ear-piercing alarm. If the thief doesn't put the attaché down quickly, a powerful and disabling electrical charge will soon surge through his body.

Sears and RadioShack sell a boat horn small enough to fit in a purse, fanny pack, or backpack. About the size of a travel-size shaving cream aerosol, it has a plastic horn attached. It costs less than ten dollars, but it's nearly as loud as an eighteen-wheeler's air horn. If you need crime-influencing attention in an emergency, you'll surely get it with the boat horn.

Learn To "Power" Yell

A scream is a weak sister compared to a power yell. A scream is often compulsive and panic-driven. The power yell is controlled, vibrant, and the loudest noise a human can make. The yell comes from deep inside. You have to practice this yell to get it right. You yell as long as it's to your advantage. The moment it isn't, or a gun or knife is the penalty if you don't stop, then you can alter your response and try another approach.

Communication Systems

Another weapon is a communication system. A cellular telephone is the best weapon you can have. If you have one, take it with you whenever possible. Since the phone itself could be a crime target, you should keep the instrument in a book bag or purse. Unfortunately, many schools do not allow students to carry cellular phones. Incoming calls are disruptive. Many of the young people who first used them at school were dope dealers taking their next illegal order. Unless you are walking through a metal detector each day, however, you can carry your cellular unit undetected if you turn it off for all incoming calls.

In other words, you can call out during an emergency. Now don't misunderstand. The mere possession of a cellular phone is often against school policy. Certainly, you can't receive any personal calls while at school, but I would rather be administratively sanctioned and safe than not be safe. When you walk past the gangbangers, your cell phone will be there with you. A personal communication system is very reassuring—even for a police officer. Get one if you can.

If someone bothers you on the way to or from school, all you need to do is dial your emergency number. Call the cellular equivalent to 911 in most dialing districts in the U.S. for immediate police, fire, or ambulance service. Just calling out can decrease your risk if someone is bothering you. The person sees you make the call and leaves before officers arrive.

No Weapons or Pepper Spray

I do not—ever—recommend that a young person carry a knife or a gun. It is against the law. It is wrong. The crook's weapon, if there is one, is one too many. A weapon at school is like death looking for a place to happen. Some crime-prevention authorities recommend small canisters of tear gas or pepper gas spray. I don't! There are several problems with these weapons. The first is the law. In some states the civilian use of spray is illegal. In most schools you could be suspended or expelled for carrying a spray device. The second problem is that these devices are not all they are cracked up to be.

While police officers use spray devices, theirs are three or four times more potent than the commercial stuff sold at your mall. The manufacturers of these materials do not tell you that tear gas and pepper spray have a short shelf life. That tear gas canister your mom has been carrying on her key ring for the last five years was "dead" at least 3½ years ago. It has a probable shelf life of no more than 1½ years. If it was stored on a warehouse shelf for any length of time, it could have been useless the day she bought it. Also, the gas spray gives her a false sense of security. She thinks, *If I get in trouble, I will spray the robber or rapist with it.*

What she ought to be doing and what you ought to be doing is avoiding the threat and the risk. You should be observing your environment and leaving the area if anything makes you feel uncomfortable. You should not say, "I will spray the sorry contemptible excuse for humanity with pepper spray! That will teach him!" What you will probably do is just make him mad.

Most of the gas and spray manufacturer advertising claims are questionable. Some gas manufacturers claim their product will "incapacitate him for fifteen to thirty minutes." That is advertising hype. Spray doesn't work that well. Ask almost any police officer about the times he used it and it didn't work, and remember his is three or four times more powerful. If you must insist on carrying a spray, though I would strongly discourage it, buy the same stuff police officers carry. Almost all large cities have a police supply store or two, or call your police department and get a toll-free telephone number so you can order what you need.

Instead of a spray, use a portable alarm. Keep fresh batteries in it. Use an air horn, or a good quality police whistle. You can always use a power yell! Then run from your trouble. Depending on yourself, your observational skills, your running ability, and your power yell is much more useful than fishing around in your purse or backpack looking for a device that may not work the day you need it the most.

chapter 7

Traveling Safely

Charles and his sister Susan live in an inner-city apartment. They live only three blocks from their school, but since they reside in a high-crime area, they must walk through two gang turfs, an illegal drug sales market, and a group of prostitutes every day. They are really apprehensive about their safety. Some of their friends have been mugged. They are always concerned and sometimes frightened. They are very careful every day.

They wear school uniforms and carry book bags. They never stare at the creeps, MICAs and prostitutes. Sometimes they walk past cars where these girls are selling sex. They never stare—nor should you—but they are aware of everything going on around them.

If you live in a nice suburb and your school is right down the street, choosing your school travel route may not be a major decision. However, if you live in the inner city or in a rough neighborhood, your route to and from school may be your most important daily decision. Guys cruising for adventure, gang members, drug pushers, prostitutes, perverts, or kidnappers could be an everyday issue in your neighborhood or in anybody's neighborhood. All of these security risks should be avoided whenever possible.

Many teens become victims because they are in the wrong place at the wrong time. Are you in a risky location because you must be? Do you have any alternatives, or did you make a bad decision? Your daily route plan is very important. Sometimes you might want to avoid a trap and vary your route and/or the time of your entry or departure. These are decisions you can control.

Some threats are predictable. Others are spontaneous. A *predictable threat* is one you know about. You should know where the gangsters, wannabees, prostitutes, or drug pushers hang out, so you try to avoid those locations. Walk another route, even if this decision makes you walk farther. If you don't want to appear

> Choosing your route to school may be the single most important security decision you will make each day.

afraid, walk to the grocery store on an adjacent street. Buy a candy bar or something. Do anything to justify walking another way. Do whatever it takes to keep your pocketbook, and dignity, and to maintain your safety. Follow the directions of Jesus, when he warned his followers, "Behold, I send you out as sheep in the midst of wolves. Therefore be wise as serpents and harmless as doves. But beware of men . . ." (Matt. 10:16–17a).

A *spontaneous threat* is one that surprises you. You walk the same way you have for years, and all at once, you are confronted with something that frightens you. Perhaps it is a homeless person with mental problems, a drunk, somebody high on drugs, a gang member, or a rapist. Whatever the threat is, avoid it. Your original avoidance plan didn't work today, so you must (as they say in the military) take countermeasures. The best countermeasure a young person can take is to run. You take countermeasures because you've been alerted. The most important difference between crime victims and nonvictims is that nonvictims stay poised and alert, ready to avoid high-risk threats.

> The best crime countermeasure a young person can take is to run. Some run and yell at the same time. A power yell can be heard for blocks.

A spontaneous threat is more likely to occur when you are alone, preoccupied with personal problems, or tired. Students who are under the influence of alcohol or drugs are the most vulnerable of all. Fatigue, personal problems, alcohol, and drugs all serve to make you less attentive and help to confuse you. These factors also increase your chances of getting lost.

Choose a Familiar Route

Always choose a familiar route. Check out alternative routes with family or friends if you are unfamiliar with adjacent territory. Never risk getting lost in a hostile neighborhood. Getting lost contributes to psychological vulnerability. It increases the chances that you can't influence the environment and the risk of being surprised by an individual thief or an entire gang. Being in unfamiliar territory also increases the risk of being isolated from your friends and your escape routes.

After deciding your route, you must also take charge of all other activities that influence your security. Let's say you are walking to school or to the bus stop. You must do two things simultaneously. First, you should walk in the middle of the sidewalk unless you have a safety reason not to. This keeps you from being surprised by someone in an alleyway, a door, or in a car.

Second, you should walk in the opposite direction of traffic. This means that cars are coming toward you. So if a creep wants you to ride with him, get away from him by continuing to walk forward. He (or she) must back up, go forward, make a U-turn, or traverse the block. Any of these options are in your favor. If you walk with the flow of traffic, somebody can drive by, grab you from behind, and pull you into a panel van. If the van is soundproofed, nobody will even hear you scream.

YOU ARE PSYCHOLOGICALLY VULNERABLE IF YOU ARE

- Lost
- Inattentive
- Preoccupied
- Confused
- Tired
- Under influence of alcohol
- Under influence of drugs

When you walk facing traffic, you are also more protected from the drunk or the driver who just had a heart attack. By facing traffic, your ability to anticipate a risk and get out of the way is

> Always walk facing traffic. Cars will be coming toward you in this position. You can always see them. You can also see a people threat.

increased. If an out-of-control vehicle is coming from behind and makes no unusual noise to alert you, it could easily turn you into fresh roadkill.

You Always Have Alternatives

You always have alternatives. If you see a creep walking toward you, cross the street for a time, and then get back on the "safest side." The safe side changed when the MICA, the gangbanger, or the creep showed up on your side. If it is late and there isn't much traffic, you can walk in the street itself. This gives you a lot more room to maneuver if someone attacks. If it's an emergency, walk (or run) in the street even if the traffic is heavy. There may be less risk from traffic than from the thug who wants to attack you.

As you observe your environment carefully, you should avoid all blind spots and recessed doorways. As you walk near an alley entrance, listen for vehicles both in the street and the alley. If it is safe to do so, you could even walk into the street in a semicircular pattern. Your destination, of course, is the sidewalk on the other side of the alley. Also, avoid large shrubs, trees, and dumpsters. Give them a wide berth. Your

intention is to remain
safe, avoiding any unac-
ceptable risk or surprise.

Try not to look
directly into the sun. Stay
in the shade so you can
see others clearly. It is
best to walk where you
can observe others, not
necessarily where they

YOU ARE MORE VULNERABLE IF YOU ARE
• Lost
• Isolated
• Immobilized
• Accessible
• Without an escape route

can easily observe you. This is a part of your avoidance
plan: learning avoidance techniques *before* your crime,
so you are fully prepared. Most victims become victims because they were caught by surprise, didn't
know what to do, and were so terrified that they
couldn't think or respond. They lost by default. If you
plan for the worst possible events, you will not lose by
default.

Be especially careful when the street is deserted.
Let's say you see few pedestrians and very little traffic.
If anyone asks for directions, listen to your feelings. If
this person gives you the creeps or makes you suspicious, continue to walk on. Under these circumstances,
it's not necessary for you to be polite to adults.
Courtesy is not in the Ten Commandments! There is
no "Holy Responsibility" to always be polite. "Safety
before courtesy," is a good rule. If you decide to help
someone with directions, stand in the middle of the
sidewalk while telling the person how to get to their
destination. Do not (by do not, I mean *NEVER*)
approach the car or lean over the window to give the
person this information. This is a good rule for all

students of either sex. Keep the distance advantage and you will avoid the trap. If there was no trap, no harm has been done.

If you feel that someone is stalking you, turn all the way around. This motion is called a "six o'clock" in the military services. A 180-degree turnaround gives you the opportunity to fully see your potential assailant. Don't just look sideways or watch someone sideways with your peripheral vision. Gavin DeBecker, in *The Gift of Fear: Survival Signals that Protect Us From Violence,* wrote: "It is better to turn completely, take in everything and look squarely at someone who concerns you. This not only gives *you information* but it *communicates to him* that you are not a tentative, frightened victim-in-waiting. You are an animal of nature, fully endowed with the hearing, sight, intellect and dangerous defenses. *You are not easy prey, so don't act like you are."*[1]

Whenever someone asks for directions, change for a parking meter, or a light for a cigarette, listen to your instincts. Leave quickly if you have a bad feeling. Don't process the feeling, or even think about it. Don't analyze the situation. Just leave! Hurting someone's feelings is preferable to being attacked or being hurt physically or emotionally.

In their book *The 7 Steps to Personal Safety* Tim Powers and Richard Isaacs wrote, "You need *distance,* about 12' or more in a public place. With friends a polite distance is 4' to 12'." Friends usually grant a personal space of 2' to 4'. Intimates like boyfriends and girlfriends allow direct contact or close contact, say no more than 2'.[2]

YOU ARE SAFER IF YOU

- Walk with others
- Walk near the center of the sidewalk
- Stay away from hiding places
- Walk facing traffic
- Scan traffic and sidewalk both front and back
- Keep moving
- Walk erect
- Make eye contact with passersby
- Control your facial expressions
- Have a neutral expression
- Are careful when lending aid
- Keep cash out of sight
- Keep cash readily available
- Stay in well-lit areas

The average attacker can cover 5' in 1/4th of a second, 10' in under 3/4th of a second and 21' in a second and a half.[3] This is not a lot of time to react, especially since most attackers seldom tip their hand until they are ready to strike. They act in a nonthreatening manner until the precise moment they attack.

Watch the people walking toward you. Their motions are called *kinesics*. Reaching for a knife or making a fist is a threatening motion and falls within the study of kinesics. *Proxemics* relates to distance and the study of distance. Maintain a safe distance from others, especially those who may appear threatening. This is called "a circle of safety." Some authorities refer to a cushion of space, a boundary, or a comfort zone. These terms are synonymous. This distance gives you time to react, maneuver, and respond. You will be much safer when you keep this rule.

Take Your Friends with You: Form Crime-Avoidance Partnerships

Everybody needs a friend. When the early apostles went on mission trips, they traveled with fellow Christians, exemplifying a protection pact between friends. Paul, Barnabas, Mark, and Titus frequently traveled together, lowering the likelihood of attack.

You also need the right kinds of friends. Let's say that Johnny and Robert live nearby. They would be naturals for forming a protection pact. However, if Johnny sells or uses drugs or if Robert is the neighborhood bully, they both stand a strong chance of being attacked wherever they go. If you are with either of these boys, you may be attacked too.

Pick some good friends to accompany you. The walk rules are the same when several young people are involved. Insofar as possible, avoid gang turfs, and stay away from dumpsters and alleys. Some additional rules apply to females. If two or more girls are walking, they should put their purses to the inside; that is, the girl on the left should carry her purse to the right, and the girl on the right should carry her purse to the left.

The purses should be touching or at least close.

THE SCIENCE OR STUDY OF MOTION AND DISTANCE
- Kinesics
- Proxemics

This placement deters both the mugger and the purse snatcher. The purse to the outside gives him direct access, a way to get to you and away from you without knocking you or your friend down. When you carry to the inside, he will have to assault you both to get one or both purses. He probably won't attempt this unless he thinks you have a big bankroll. Your purse flap should also face toward you, making it more difficult for a pickpocket. In cold weather, put your coat on over your purse, which is already looped around your shoulder.

Do the same thing with wallets. Put them to the inside, or carry your wallet in your jacket pocket or in a snug-fit-

> You are always more vulnerable when you are alone.

ting front trouser pocket. Many crime-conscious students sew velcro in their pockets and on their wallets. Others put a pocket comb lengthwise in the fold of their wallet with the teeth pointed up. If someone attempts to pick your pocket or jerk your wallet out, the comb gets stuck. Inside your wallet, the comb is pretty strong, so it's not likely to break.

Friends can help prevent crime for each other and for themselves. You are always more vulnerable when you are alone. Being alone is the single factor most often associated with crime. If you are not alone, you are less vulnerable. One San Francisco crime study showed that walking with one other person reduces your chance of becoming a victim by 67 percent. Two or more friends walking together lowers your chances of being victimized by 90 percent.[4] Go to school or the bus stop with your friends. Plan your routes ahead of time and travel together.

Even though you are lessening your likelihood of becoming a crime victim when you travel with your friends, you still should stay alert. There is an unusual group phenomenon known as "group paralysis." Each group member waits for another group member to do something. When nobody moves, the collective response is to do nothing. The same thing happens to individuals, but psychologists call it "frozen fright" when applying it to an individual.

This "paralysis" doesn't need to happen to you. Since you are observing your environment, analyzing what you observe, and reacting to your observations, you may react more quickly than any of your friends. Exert leadership and direction here for your friends. Tell them what to do, and set the example by doing it yourself! Nonvictims act to remove themselves from danger quickly. You decrease your chances of being a victim when you control your actions and reactions.

Using School and Public Rest Rooms

John saw them and knew they didn't belong. They were too old to be fellow students, but instead of exiting quickly and using another rest room, he went in anyway. He obeyed the security rules by going into a stall and locking the door. However, as he exited, one big fellow grabbed him and pushed his face into a toilet filled with water. Struggling for breath, John couldn't prevent a second guy from taking his wallet. The third thief served as a door lookout.

John made a serious judgment error when he decided to stay in the rest room. Had he returned quickly to the hallway, he would have been safer.

You would think that most rest rooms are safe, but, in fact, they are like magnets. Rest rooms attract undesirables, thieves, perverts, and rapists. Public rest rooms inside busy buildings are safer than the lonely, rarely used facility with an outside access door.

Most modern service stations and fast food restaurants have rest rooms on the inside, which are safer than rest rooms with outside entrances. Outside rest rooms should be avoided whenever possible. Should you have an emergency, you can leave your friends outside while you go in. If several crime-avoidance partners are with you, leave some outside and take the others in with you. This is another good example of security partnerships.

When you open the door of any rest room, look around carefully for any threats. A large, busy rest room is safer. Creeps and thieves are less likely to bother you when others are there. Hold on to your possessions while you are in the rest room.

Males are extremely vulnerable in a public rest room. Facing the urinal, your back is to the open area and to your assailant. In dangerous areas, use the private cubicles. Some boys always use the cubicle, even to the point of sitting to urinate, rather than turning their back on strangers. However, you are vulnerable at the moment when you are pulling your trousers up or down, so this is not always the best alternative. If your buddy is with you, take turns using the toilet or urinal. You watch for danger while your buddy is distracted.

Girls, do not put your purse on the floor when you sit on the toilet. Hold it in your lap, or loop it over a clothing hook. If someone asks you for toilet paper or to return something she dropped, push it over with your foot and bring your foot back to the center of the toilet cubicle quickly. Do not hand the item to the person. If the person is a thief or a pervert, she might grab your hand. You could be pulled off balance and onto the rest room floor.

Bus or Subway Travel

Plan for bus or subway travel just as you would your walk to school. One of the best rules is to minimize your waiting time. If a bus comes by your favorite stop every fifteen minutes on a reasonably

---

WAITING FOR THE BUS OR SUBWAY

- Wait with others.
- Minimize your wait.
- Stand away from the road/rail.
- Have change or token ready.
- Be confident when boarding.
- See who is aboard.
- Sit near driver or operator.
- Sit where you can see.
- Sit near an aisle.
- Sit near an exit.
- Don't sit by anyone who seems out of place or who gives you the creeps.
- Stay away from MICAs.

precise schedule, then you can time your wait for just three or four minutes instead of ten or fifteen. The bus stop is another "magnet" for thieves and rapists. As you wait, use the buddy rule. Wait with other people, preferably friends of yours.

Keep crime-avoidance partnerships intact. Each of you is safer because the other is there. It is really nice when an older teenager or adult can accompany you. Such a person is often called a *guardian.* Never assume, however, that adult strangers or others will come to your aid if or when you get in trouble. There are no guarantees. In criminal attacks, you may well face your crime

> Don't ride this particular bus or subway if anyone or anything gives you the creeps.

all alone, even though others are physically present. They may be immobilized, frightened, or perhaps will choose to mind their own business.

Keep your bus fare or token handy. Don't let everyone around see how much cash you have. If you have planned ahead, you just reach for your token or the correct change.

If you must buy a ticket or a token at a station and somebody creepy gets in line behind you, deal with the problem quickly. You could turn around and ask the person, "Are you going to buy a ticket?" I know you would prefer not to talk to him at all, but this is the safest thing to do. If the answer is, "Yes, I'm buying a ticket," then say, "Go on ahead of me, please. My bus/tram/subway doesn't leave for a while." You need to stand *behind* suspicious persons. Don't let them stand behind you. In some cities, particular tokens or tickets let the creep know where you are going. By letting him purchase his ticket and leave, you deprive him of this information.

As you board, look at the passengers. If anyone gives you the creeps, get off before you pay, or drop your token in the receptacle. Don't sit near anyone you feel uneasy about. Sit as close to the driver as you can. *The nearer the driver, the safer you are.* Sit where you can see, and sit near an exit. An aisle seat is safer than a window seat because you can't be blocked in by a creep. Girls are less likely to be accidentally-on-purpose pawed by a disgusting pervert.

Observe your stop carefully before you exit. If you see anything that bothers you, don't get off. Take the next safe exit, or travel to the end of the line and get off on the way back. You can control your schedule even if someone is stalking you or a predator is waiting. Most creeps won't wait that long.

Riding in a Taxi

Never take maverick or unlicensed taxis. They may be cheaper, but they aren't regulated by the police or safety inspectors, so you are at a higher risk. Pick a distinctive cab with a well-known company. If possible, use the buddy system. Take someone else with you instead of traveling alone.

Never get in a cab with a stranger as a fellow passenger. An unknown driver and the unknown fare increase your risk. If someone else gets into the cab after you, get out quickly. You are paying for a ride by yourself, not a group rate.

Tell your driver where you are going and the fastest way to get there. If he takes another route or gives you the creeps, get out at your next opportunity. If you have the cellular phone recommended previously, call and tell your mom

> The nearer the driver, the safer you are.

what cab you are in (the number is usually posted on the dashboard) and when you plan to arrive. This call increases your safety. You can do this casually, not as if you distrust your driver. Just say, "Hi Mom, I'm running late again. I am at _____ (give your approximate location) in cab _____ (give the taxi company name and the city cab license number posted on the dashboard). I'll be arriving at approximately _____ (give your approximate arrival time)."

You can use a widely applied security method at the pickup address. With the driver watching you, write down the number of the cab and give it to a friend before you get into the cab. If there are two car-loads of folks going in the same direction, both sets of cab occupants should exchange cab numbers. This is like an accounting audit. It helps keep everyone honest. Adults should do this too. It helps keep all passengers safe from the perils of crime.

If You Drive

Your car can help you escape from trouble, but it can also get you into serious difficulty; it can also be a trap. The car can be the target itself. Some automobile and truck models are more frequently hijacked.

Some guy walks up to you with a gun and takes your car away from you. Sometimes he takes you with it. Most cars are hijacked between 10:00 PM and 2:00 AM when fewer people are around to intrude or to serve as guardians. Get home before midnight and drive on well-traveled and well-lit roads. Avoid twenty-four-hour self-serve stores after dark. After-hours shopping increases the hijacking, mugging, robbery, kidnap and rape risk, so fill up your car with gasoline in the daytime. Buy your bread at the same time. Avoid car-wash facilities and self-serve stores after daylight hours.

Here is how you can lessen your risk while in route. Let's say you are traveling down a four-lane street. The safest lane is the inside lane nearest the center of the street. Quite often drivers are attacked at intersections. Don't drive right up behind the car in front of you. Give yourself room to evade any attacker. Leave at least a car-length space between your car and the vehicle in front of you.

Let's say that you are stuck in traffic at a stoplight. If your car is two feet behind the car in front of you and someone else is up against your rear bumper, then you are stuck. However, if you leave yourself room to maneuver and are in the inside lane when the thief intrudes, you can still take off. You can get in the wrong lane, make a U-turn, drive past other cars against the light, or run up the street against the flow of traffic, blowing your horn and blinking your emergency flashers all the way. Even if you must go slowly, you can still go. If you can't move your car, you are stuck, and you are already a victim.

If you keep a cellular phone with you at all times, you can use it now. If you don't have one, buy a realistic-looking toy phone at the mall for two dollars and pretend to call. This may be sufficient to prevent an intrusion.

Let's say you are driving to a school function at your local mall. Your school's choral group is going to sing at a common-access area. What should you do to ensure your safety? First, you should park carefully. When you get to the mall parking lot, drive around it at least once. Watch for any threats to your safety. If you see any potential risks, move to another area of the mall parking lot, or come back later. When you do park, be sure that no obstructions block your vision. Make sure you can see any threat before you exit your car and before you reenter it. Wherever possible, back into your parking place. At night, park in a well-lit area. Keep your car locked, and make sure your valuables are not exposed. Leave them in the trunk.

When you return to your car, try not to be restricted by carrying too many packages. It is better to make more trips than to be overly burdened by your recent purchases. As you exit the store for the parking

---

WHEN DRIVING

- Drive near the center of the street.
- At traffic lights, keep plenty of distance between your front bumper and the car in front of you.
- If someone bothers you, start honking, turn on your hazard lights, and call 911 on your cell phone.

PARKING HINTS

- Park away from visual obstructions.
- Park away from vans.
- At night, park in well-lit areas.
- Avoid occupied vehicles.
- As a pedestrian, avoid cars in motion.
- As you walk to your car, look under it and behind the seat before entering.
- Stay alert—your life depends on it.

lot, scan the parking area for threats to your safety. You may be tired, but you need to stay alert. Look out for moving vehicles. Other vehicles may be threats as well. Move over a lane if someone is driving near you. As you approach your car, try to see under it. Recently, some thieves and rapists have hidden under cars. They grab their victims by the ankles and pull them down prior to robbery and/or rape. If you feel threatened or intimidated in any way, find a security officer to walk with you. He will be glad to help.

Looking under your car as you approach it, avoiding moving vehicles, walking around other vehicles, and avoiding vehicles that are occupied will increase your safety and lessen your risk. Also, you should be especially careful about vans. Stay away from them whenever possible. That side door and the darkened glass could be your trap "said the spider to the fly."

Be wary if you discover a flat tire, especially if the tire is new and in good condition. Someone may have punctured it or removed your air-valve core. If your car won't crank even though it was running perfectly

when you parked, consider the possibility that someone has sabotaged your car. Be especially wary of the
nice stranger who suddenly appears out of nowhere
and is interested in helping you. *You* should pick the
person to help. Don't let a stranger pick you.

Riding Your Bike

Always take your bike lock with you. In most cities
the bike won't be there when you come back if it is not
secured. While riding, always remember to wear your
safety helmet. It will protect you from traffic accidents
and personal assaults as well. If someone attacks, duck
your head and take the blow on the helmet. An incoming blow won't hurt you, but it sure will damage your
attacker's fist.

You can always ditch the bike and run in a rural
setting, but a mountain bike should take you anywhere—in ditches, up and down curbs, on sidewalks,
and between parked cars. Don't ride fast near pedestrians and pay special attention to safety issues, but ride
like the wind when threatened.

When you can, ride with friends who are dependable riders, not local thugs or gangsters. Bad company
will always get you into their fight. If gangsters try to
cut you off, don't panic. Always be looking for alternate routes, even between houses, lots, and alleys. Just
don't get trapped in a dead end.

chapter 8

Avoiding Troublemakers

Some of the students at Cindy's high school can only be described as "really strange" young people. Since there hasn't been much violence at Richville High, the principals have allowed students to "do their own thing." There are no color or clothing restrictions. The Richville mayor, chamber of commerce, city manager, and chief of police all claim, "Richville doesn't have troubles with youth gangs, drugs, and deviant cults." However, Cindy questions this statement because she sees black lipstick and nail polish on students holding *Satanic Bibles*.

Cindy also knows that several students are selling drugs on campus and that one group of students has formed a group called the "Outlaws." Rumor has it that an applicant must commit a theft or some other serious crime prior to being considered for membership. Yesterday Cindy saw a pistol grip sticking out from the belt of the vice president of the Outlaws.

The authorities may tell you that everything is all right at your school, but your mind tells you that things do not look all right. You need to determine the truth about security at your school. How do you recognize those who might threaten your safety, and how can you avoid them?

Who Are the Troublemakers?

Some troublemakers are easy to spot. They dress like troublemakers, and they act like troublemakers. Others are as hard to find as an undercover narcotic agent or a spy in the Central Intelligence Agency.

If you see a homeless woman coming toward you pushing a grocery cart filled with junk, you might choose to take precautions. The same is true for a staggering drunk or someone strung out on drugs. One avoidance method would be to move to the opposite side of the walk. Another might be to cross the street. Still another might be to duck into a store or business, watching as the person walks by. The MICA, the homeless woman, the drunk, and the street person whose mind has been drug-burned are all easily recognized.

TROUBLEMAKERS

- Truants and tardy students
- Weapon carriers
- Bullies
- Gang members
- Drug traffickers and substance abusers
- Ritualistic groups
- Vigilantes

These deviants are not authorized to be in your school. However, several other types of potentially dangerous people, both students and nonstudents, do frequent your school. They are visible because they wear "colors," bandannas, and jackets that identify them. Sometimes the color, or even the angle a baseball cap is tilted, signals that its wearer is a gang member. Your most visible school risk is the gang member. Members of violent gangs are "death looking for a place to happen." There are, however, other less visible potential troublemakers.

Truants and Tardy Students

Unhappy or academically marginal students are often called *dysfunctional* by the education community. These are the students who cause over 90 percent of all school problems. Five to six percent of all teenagers and young boys commit half or more of all serious crimes, according to Professor James Q. Wilson of UCLA,[1] so the troublemakers should be watched.

Students who skip class frequently are normally the biggest troublemakers at school. Frequent absenteeism and tardiness is one major "troublemaker" predictor. Statistics indicate that students who miss between five and fifty class periods each year commit most of the serious school offenses.[2] High school freshman and sophomore students tend to commit more offenses, as do those students with lower grade point averages. Males commit more offenses than females. Beware of these potential troublemakers.

Weapon Carriers

A small percentage of students today are carrying weapons to school. While fewer guns are seized by police than other types of weapons, we are seeing a significant increase in gun-related school crimes. Any weapon is a significant threat to your well-being at school. Brass or aluminum knuckles, knives (including fiberglass knives that will pass through metal detector scrutiny), black-jacks, razors, box cutters, and chemical irritants are all examples of school weapons.

Students carry weapons for a variety of reasons. Some think it gives them a mystique or some macho status. Others intend to steal, rob, or rape using the weapon for intimidation. Others are good students who are tired of being pushed around and don't want to be intimidated again. They don't want to use their weapons, but they don't want to be the only ones without weapons.

The firearm is the most lethal of all weapons. You are much more likely to survive a stabbing than a gunshot, but all weapons are potentially deadly. Please keep weapons out of your school. Keeping weapons, drugs, and alcohol out of your school is vital to your security.

Bullies

Many teenagers are afraid of particular bullies. Virtually every classroom and every school is affected by bullying. Over eight hundred thousand students nationwide skip school each day because they are afraid to go.[3] One out of every twelve students who quits school at an early age stops going because he or she is afraid to go.[4] These students are literally pushed out of school. They don't drop out for traditional academic failure or economic reasons; they abandon their studies because they are scared to death.[5] Some of the students who are frequently absent are skipping school because they are afraid, not because they are delinquent. Bullyied victims are left with psychological scars that last years after the intimidation stops.

Male bullies are usually larger than their victims. One rather unusual statistic reveals that female bullies are usually smaller than the students they pick on. They simply use the power of their personalities and are willing to use force to intimidate less aggressive students. Both male and female bullies feel a need to intimidate, force, and control the behavior of others. They are sadistic. Sadism is a deviancy in which the bully gets pleasure from scaring, intimidating, or hurting another person. Most bullies enjoy administering abuse, but abusing others also causes them problems. Sometimes kids abused for years outgrow their bullies and seek revenge. At any rate, violence spirals wherever bullies operate.

Bullies are a problem all students must encounter. Helping bullies learn how to handle conflict is an important effort because a large percentage of bullies go to prison. Bullies can usually be spotted by their eighth year. The more aggressive eight-year-old is very likely to come into frequent police contact as a teenager and an adult. Aggressive boys are less likely to finish college or to have good jobs. Aggressive girls grow up to be the mothers of bullies.

If bullies can learn how to resolve conflict and not push people around, they may avoid the penalties. If they can learn not to menace, they might even be able to compete and succeed in our society. However, if they don't learn these lessons, they'll not succeed. In fact, bullies are three times more likely to be jailed than their friends. In the meantime, they are harming others.

Gang Members

Schools were once believed to be a neutral zone, relatively immune from gang violence. Now schools are frequently used as recruiting stations and turf war battlegrounds. Let's create a fictitious group. We will call this gang the CGG (the Covenant Garden Gang), named after a gang from a local apartment complex. Gang members associated with this group may now claim that, "The CGG is in charge of this school." Gangs cause a higher school drop-out rate. They frequently rob students, taking their lunch and bus money. Other students are often coerced into joining the gang, or they suffer the consequences of frequent fights and intimidation.

Being in the presence of a gang member increases your risk of violence. You are not as safe as you could be just because a gang member is there. If a rival gang member sees you with him, you could easily experience a "drive-by" shooting. Even a fistfight may have more serious consequences for onlookers because of the extreme violence.

Gang members are usually recruited between the ages of eleven and fifteen. Some street gangs recruit boys between the age of eight and twelve. Gang members begin to gain strength and confidence while they are still in middle school or in junior high. They stay in the gang until their twenties. Sometimes they can't leave. Too sudden a departure may be construed as betrayal. Gang peers may believe that those departing members have become police informants or that they have flipped (surreptitiously joined another gang). Sometimes gang members never leave, retaining lifetime membership. School officials unaware of the gang problem often tolerate their presence, never realizing that today's gangs constitute an organized criminal effort.

Contrary to popular belief, gangs are not restricted to minorities or to kids from disadvantaged neighborhoods. Gang members represent all racial and ethnic groups. Many middle-class and upper-class youth are involved in gang activity.

Gang members like to strut. They are looking for attention. They appear menacing and increase the menace with sheer numbers, preferring to walk in groups of no less than three, but usually with five to ten clearly distinguishable members. Some call it a gang "shuffle." Their numbers, in or out of school, are intimidating. Sometimes the larger gangs are referred to as "wolf packs." It is a very appropriate description.

Dr. Ronald Stevens, Director of the National School Safety Center, says that "Today's gangs pose a greater threat than at any time in recent history." Gangs are presently within the boundaries of virtually every school district in the United States. Gangs are no longer just a boys' or girls' social club. Many gangs are formed for protecting the membership. Other gangs are formed exclusively for profit through criminal activity. Their primary crime is usually drug sales or drug control in your neighborhood.

In other cases, gangs "extort" (take by force, intimidate, or frighten children and young people into giving them protection money). For the privilege of using the restroom, a hallway, a sidewalk, or the cafeteria, the unmolested young person must pay a "permission tax." Young children and loners are extorted most often. The kids who don't pay are harassed, abused, and attacked. Older and larger students are usually left alone.

Rebellious lifestyles have always existed. Long hair, mustaches, boy's earrings, and clothing styles were issues in the past. Today the primary issue is the gang itself, but gang colors, gang caps (and the way the caps are worn), gang jackets, graffiti, signing (gang sign language), and drugs are the alternate issues. Sometimes gangs wear the jackets of particular professional sports teams as well as team caps or shirts. This was first done to help gang members blend in at school and in the street, but the symbolism is the same—it often means *gang*.

Starter jackets can become dangerous as well. Joe Lee is not very observant. He also has the same favorite team as the local Gangster Disciples, or the Urban Thugs. When Joe wears his new jacket to school, four things could happen. First, he could be associated with the gang. If there is to be a "rumble," he could easily be caught up in it. Second, the gang may be angry that he is wearing *their jacket* when he is not a member.

Third, a Gangster Disciple is much more likely to steal Joe Lee's jacket. Fourth, an opposing gang may single Joe out for retribution over some past event.

Sometimes a community or a school experiences so much violence that young people join opposing gangs just to get the protection of gang membership. These prospective members want protection and influence. Gang power and influence is called "juice" in the gang community.

Many, if not most, gang members come from dysfunctional homes. The gang becomes a substitute support group for traditional parental care. The gang offers friendship, self-esteem, status, rank, and money. Never forget that they use some forms of crime to profit from their gang association. Financial gain continues to be a powerful motive for gang involvement, especially in poorer neighborhoods. Middle-class

---

WHAT CAN YOU DO?

- Display friendly attitudes toward other students and teachers.
- Dress for success! Wear clean, inexpensive clothes, and inexpensive jewelry.
- Students should not wear hairstyles identifying themselves as gang members.
- Students should not wear gang colors.
- Students should not wear gang jewelry.
- Students should not wear gang tatoos or brands.
- Students should not use gang signals.
- Do not allow gang graffiti at your school. *Students* go to school. Gang members can associate elsewhere.

kids, however, need more money if they are doing drugs. Even rich kids overspend and may join for the cash.

At the extreme, however, the gang creates servitude. Gang members do what the gang bosses say to do. You keep "their" schedules, not yours. Some gangs do not and will not let you quit. You can't resign or retire. In some urban neighborhoods, three and four generations of a gang live in a single household. Often the only way out of the gang is death! Because of this danger, gangs should always be prohibited, especially at school.

If your school doesn't have these rules now, you should ask your student government to pass them as formal policy and request that your school administration or school board accept them as well.

Gang Graffiti

Graffiti is one form of gang art. It communicates that a gang claims a particular territory. If someone paints gang symbols on a school wall, the artwork should be removed that same day.

Paintbrushes and paint should always be available. Students who have misbehaved or were tardy should be made to stay after school to paint over the graffiti each day.

If a student is caught spray painting or wall drawing, the school should require him to clean all of the graffiti for the next month or so. Repeat offenders should be turned over to the police for arrest and prosecution.

Some schools have Campus Pride campaigns. Student graffiti artists, wall drawers, and wall poets are challenged to compete in the design of acceptable slogans and posters used to encourage a positive atmosphere. The best artwork, in drawings, painting, and spray-art, is given awards and ribbons. The campus poets are also rewarded, and their work is published in school newsletters and in the school annual.

Keeping a school clean will make it safer. Gangs use the graffiti to establish "no trespassing" areas on their own turfs. If they ever establish control, then all nonmembers are at risk, even teachers and school staff. Removing the graffiti denies them "their" space and opens the areas for the use of everyone.

If your school staff is still in denial—that is, they still do not believe that gangs operate at your school—you may be the one who alerts them to the fact that there is a real problem. Denial, camouflaging, and downplaying are standard administrative reactions to gang problems. "We don't have gang problems at our school" is a typical denial reaction, especially when the gangs are clearly in evidence. With this administrative approach of looking the other way,

> Gang symbols and artwork should be removed quickly. The symbols establish a gang territory.

the gangs are getting ever stronger. Conscientious students must alert parents and school authorities. Let them know that there *is* a problem.

Substance Abusers

The Federal Office of Juvenile Justice Delinquency Prevention Research claims that the proportion of students claiming to be high on drugs or under the influence of alcohol ranges from 2.2 percent at some schools to nearly 10 percent at others. The number of students using recreational drugs is increasing all over America. At least three million teenagers are problem drinkers. The National Institute of Education's study on *Violent Schools—Safe Schools* reports that at least one in four of all high school students consume alcohol on a weekly basis and over 6 percent consume it every day.

Many students seem to believe the myth that drug abuse is a "victimless crime." They believe that the teenagers abusing drugs and alcohol are only hurting themselves. This is a lie! Nothing could be further from the truth. Drug crimes hurt the students who abuse them, and they harm the students who come into contact with the abusers. The hallucinogenic chemicals (THC levels) in marijuana have been increasing over the last three decades, so this drug is more dangerous today than in the past.

The frequent abuser is not learning at the same level as other students. Even really bright students who abuse drugs are decreasing the possibility of athletic or academic scholarships and college enrollment. When students use cocaine, crack, methamphetamine, and hallucinogenic drugs, they are gambling on their future. Usually they are gambling to lose.

Drugs and drug pushers at school are a real safety and security problem for several reasons. It takes money to buy drugs; therefore, large sums of money are exchanged at drug-sale locations. The drug pusher often feels the need to carry a weapon, either a knife or a gun, in order to keep his money safe. If he doesn't, he will be robbed. Where there are drugs, there are

---

DRUG-FREE SCHOOLS

Keep your school drug free. If the drugs are there, the money is there, and the weapons are there to protect the drugs, the money, and the pushers.

---

rip-offs. Where there are rip-offs, there is violence. Weapons, gangs, and violence proliferate in drug environments.

Keeping drugs and the gangs running or controlling the drug distribution network out of middle schools and high schools may be the single most important security measure available. No other safe-school strategy will work as well. It then becomes very important for students to become involved in working for a drug-free school environment.

SAFE SCHOOLS

Ensuring that your school is drug free is the most important thing you can do for increased safety and security.

Ritualistic Groups

The United States Constitution guarantees religious liberty. However, in recent years our government has chosen to separate religious activities from the classroom. Therefore, school authorities and students themselves should not tolerate satanic cults operating in the school environment. These aren't cute little

social clubs whose mem-
bers are just showing
their independence and
variance with societal
norms. These teenagers
believe in death, in ritualistic suicide, and some-

> ## RITUALISM BELIEFS
> Ritualistic groups believe
> in death, in ritualistic
> suicide, and in human
> sacrifice.

times in sacrificing a human offering to Satan. Usually
these "offerings" are very young children, or even a
member of their own group.

Sometimes the nerds and weirdos of your school are
attracted to ritualistic groups because they don't con-
nect with other students. Just like a gang, the ritualists offer status, group security, and a feeling of
belonging. Students who are unhappy at home, at
school, and in your community are especially likely to
be recruited.

Satanists also use graffiti. If you don't know what
to look for, you'll miss it completely. You might even
think it is just another form of street art or gang graffiti. Don't be deceived, however. It is not the same.
Once you understand how the satanic artists operate,
you may be able to interpret things you didn't understand before. Most graffiti artists put their artwork in
prominent eye-level locations, and satanists may do
the same. However, the satanist may also create his artwork in the lowest possible location on a wall. If you
say, "The artist had to lie down in the mud to draw
that," you may be looking at satanic artwork. The reason these artists draw their artwork as close to the
ground or floor as possible is that they want it to be
closer to hell and to Satan. Lower placement allows

this according to their beliefs. The numbers 666 are the centuries-old symbol of Satan worship. These numbers are probably the most frequently used ritualistic symbols.

Ritualistic violence often includes human sacrifice as well as serial suicide. When serial suicide takes place, several teenagers commit suicide within a few days of each other. Ritualists believe in a form of reincarnation. They commit suicide because they believe they are taken to a better or higher life when they die. When police begin to find burned-out candles in local cemeteries or a decapitated teenager, you can be sure there is ritualism in your community. Some even have pre-frontal lobotomies (a surgical procedure removing the brain's frontal lobe) in which they kill the victim in a formal ceremony, cut open her skull (it's a female more often than not), and offer the brain to Satan.

If you have an unusual or bizarre suicide at your school, the probability is that you will have several more. Cooperate with the police. Tell the authorities who the friends of the deceased are. You may well save a life.

Vigilantes

Vigilantes are a way of life in America. When the authorities aren't protecting society, local people step in and do it themselves. Many movies and TV shows depict the strong individual seeking revenge when the justice organizations fail to act. This concept is reinforced through our songs, rap music, movies, and TV shows. Violence is a part of our culture, and that culture is reflected at school. Probably the vigilante is

> In all probability, the vigilante is the most dangerous student at your school. The vigilante is usually a good student—just like you.

the most dangerous student at your school. If you are angry about the violence at your school, you, too, could easily become a vigilante.

Picture this scenario. Mark and Suzy are always being pushed around by the gangs or the school bully. They have been embarrassed, intimidated, stolen from, and harmed. Mark has been extorted. Gang members took his lunch money. Once a Gangster Disciple even took the watch Mark's dad gave him for Christmas. Suzy has been frequently harassed with harmful words. Billy, the bully, once leered at her and put his hand down her blouse right in front of his friends. They all laughed and thought he was cool. She was mortified, embarrassed, and ashamed. Suzy still has nightmares about the incident.

Mark and Suzy are just the types of students to seek revenge. Mark wants to get his watch back with his uncle's gun as an equalizer. Suzy hid a butcher knife in a hollowed-out section of a textbook. She plans to slash the next guy who paws her. Mark and Suzy are drawing a line in the sand. The next time they are abused, somebody will be hurt.

A school rebellion took place in Boston several years ago. Several kids left school in an ambulance. The insurrectionists were probably the nicest kids at that school. They were tired of being abused, ripped off, and bullied. The girls were tired of being groped. They were tired of getting caught in the middle of gang conflict. They were tired of the campus drug pushers. They were tired of being scared.

Their rebellion was spontaneous, overwhelming, and violent. Several drug pushers, bullies, and thugs were sent to the hospital in an ambulance. Even school officials and teachers were injured. This wasn't just a fight; it was a rebellion. School was canceled for an entire week. School administrators attended crisis management sessions to figure out what had happened. They learned that the students did not believe the adult guardians had done a good job of maintaining order, and they decided to do it themselves. The students knew the school was not safe and were angry at teachers and administrators for their negligence. These teenagers were tired of being afraid.

This is why you need to learn conflict-resolution skills and to know how to appropriately influence inappropriate conduct. The Scripture says, "A soft answer turns away wrath, But a harsh word stirs up anger" (Prov. 15:1). This is the appropriate response to conflict. Also, Proverbs says that "He who is slow to anger is better than the mighty" (Prov. 16:32). Paul, in his letter to the Ephesians, told them to "Let all bitterness, wrath, anger, clamour, and evil speaking be put away from you, with all malice" (Eph. 4:31). You need to

> When vigilantes rebel, everyone will be in danger.

learn how to handle conflict before you explode in a violent rage. Kids who continue to be abused and bullied may eventually rebel. When they do, it will be with an equalizer like a knife, a gun, or a baseball bat;

and everyone will be in danger, not just the rebels and their victims.

When we don't keep our schools safe, we "create" vigilantes who become criminals because of their reactive violence. We encourage vigilantism, because teenagers believe there is no other alternative when adult guardians have failed to keep the school safe. We create tensions for which teachers cannot compensate.

When you help the school staff ensure that your school is a "crime-free zone," that bullying is not tolerated, that the school is drug free, that student-age drug pushers must sell elsewhere during after-school hours, that the ritualists don't meet on school property, and that your school is gun free, there will be no reason for vigilantism. All will be safer because students are cooperating to create a secure environment.

chapter 9

Becoming a Successful Victim

Mike made the highest college entrance exam score in his city. He was invited to appear on a TV show honoring local scholars. Dressed in his best clothes, he headed downtown on the Z subway. Getting off at the correct stop, he walked right into trouble.

A bunch of guys wearing gangster clothes told him he had to pay them for the privilege of walking through "their" territory. Mike told them he didn't have anything, but they didn't believe him. Grabbing him from behind, they took his wallet and even his return token. Afraid that a subway police officer would come in on the next car, they ran off, leaving Mike shaken, disheveled, and broke.

It is easy to feel sorry for Mike because he was assaulted, intimidated, and robbed. Don't feel too sorry for him, however, because Mike is a "successful victim." He didn't go to the hospital, and the coroner isn't putting him into a body bag. He isn't a loser; he's a winner because he still IS. If he had lost his temper, become hysterical, or started fighting against over-whelming force, he most certainly would have been harmed or killed. Let's examine the concept of the successful victim. We can do this by studying "winners" and looking at "losers."

Winners and Losers

Just as there are winners and losers in life, there are also winners and losers in crime prevention. Some are never victimized, while those who fail in crime prevention lose their money and valuables and sometimes travel by ambulance to a hospital or in a hearse to the morgue.

Winners are successful victims. Some successful victims avoid the crime entirely. Jimmy saw the Covenant Garden Gang approaching and altered his route home. He wasn't even intimidated, much less attacked. Shirley saw a creepy guy following her. As she walked by the police officer directing traffic near her school, she told him that this stranger had been stalking her for several days. The officer investigated, and the stalker never followed her again.

Sometimes you can be a winner by just surviving. Let's say you are always as alert as a soldier in a war zone. You avoid crime and criminals. You don't wear expensive clothes or costly valuables. You never carry more money than you need to meet daily expenses. Many teenagers become victims just because they are in the wrong place at the wrong time. Sometimes this can be avoided. Sometimes it can't.

One day, two armed guys jump out of a van and rob you. How can you be successful when you have been robbed? This is a good and practical question to which there is a good answer. You can be successful by leaving, living, and surviving. The successful victim always survives.

During a Robbery

Someone puts a knife in your ribs and wants your allowance. He wants it right now! You better let him have it. Sometimes the robber is a girl, but she has a knife, a box cutter, sharp scissors, or a gun. You better let her have your allowance. The time to stop this crime occurred before she attacked. The time to stop the crime occurred when you were supposed to be observant—and weren't. Now it's too late. You've let her get too close.

> **SUCCESSFUL VICTIMS**
> - Leave
> - Live
> - Survive
> - Avoid the hospital
> - Avoid the morgue

The best advice in a robbery is to stay cool. Don't overreact. Don't get hysterical. If you get excited, the robber will too. An excited robber is more dangerous, so a hysterical reaction can easily get you killed. Whatever you do, don't scream or holler when the person with the knife is close enough to stab. Don't fight or resist when the threat of death or harm is immediate. If you can get away, do it quickly! "Flight before fight if at all possible," is a very reasonable crime-avoidance approach in any street attack.

> The best advice during a robbery is to stay cool!

Otherwise, do what the robber tells you. Comply with his wishes. Be courteous. This sounds offensive to an assertive teenager, but respect and courtesy during a robbery can save your life. This is not the occasion to tell the robber what you think of thieves, or to resist verbally in any way. Verbal or passive resistance can get you killed. Telling a robber that he is a thief or that he is evil is a quick route to the morgue. A young offender usually has a hostile response to *dis* (disrespect) and is willing to kill to guarantee respect for himself and his perceived status as a bad-guy gangster.

While your chance of being murdered is only about two out of every reported one thousand armed robberies, you must also remember that over 9 percent of all murder victims are killed during robberies. J. Edgar Hoover, the former director of the Federal Bureau of Investigation once said that an armed robbery was "like death looking for a place to happen." He knew what he was talking about. Tread lightly. Don't take unnecessary risks with your life.

Be careful. Speak distinctly and appropriately. Don't make any sudden moves, but don't move too slowly either. If your crook thinks you are passively resisting by being too slow to respond to his demands, he may explode into a maniac's rage. Victims who act too quickly are also likely to be harmed. Any resistance encourages assault, injury, and murder.

Most robbers in America are nineteen years old or even younger, as are a disproportionate percentage of all their robbery victims. They are young people stealing from other young people. An inexperienced or immature robber is much more dangerous than an experienced robber and is much more likely to use lethal force.

If you're looking down the barrel of a mean-looking pistol or are watching light reflect off the point of a dagger, stop and look at your attacker. Look in his eyes. The pistol won't go off unless he pulls the trigger. Before he slashes you, his facial features and body language will probably reflect his intentions. Speak quietly and with respect. Let him know everything is OK. You'll let him have your watch, money, or ring. This cooperation is especially important when your robber or attacker is high or obviously under the influence of alcohol.

Do exactly as the robber commands. Don't do anything he doesn't tell you to do. If he says to raise your hands, then do so carefully. If he doesn't order you to put your hands above your head, then don't assume these are his wishes. Do not speak unless you are ordered to do so. Nobody likes a smart mouth, especially a robber. Do not argue. Do not debate. Do not

---

ROBBERY TIPS

- Do exactly as the robber commands.
- Don't make any sudden movements.
- Do not speak unless you are ordered to.
- Don't risk your life for your money or other valuables.
- If a robber orders you to lie down, do so.
- Resist only if you believe he intends to kill you anyway.
- Do not attempt to follow the robber.
- Call the police after the robber leaves.

tell him how wrong he is or that robbery is an evil crime. If the robber orders you to lie down, then do so. If he says to lie there for ten minutes, this is OK too. As long as he is leaving, this is an acceptable compliance.

Whatever you do, do not follow the robber. Just let him leave. He is just as dangerous upon leaving as he was pointing his weapon at you. If he senses pursuit, he may shoot. While police officers would like to discover where your robber lives or what make of car he used in the getaway, following him is an incredibly dangerous act. When the crime is over, call the police. If it takes place at school, tell the principal after you have called the police.

Sometimes the school administration resists the police response. In fact, one study revealed that over two-thirds of all violent crimes resulting in hospitalization were not reported to the police by school authorities.[1] Another national study showed that two-thirds of all school robberies are not reported to the police.[2] In the National Institute of Education study, several years ago, it was determined that only one school crime in fifty-eight is reported to the police.[3] Do not let the principal decide whether the police will be called when a serious crime has been committed. It's your decision alone, or yours and your parents, not the principal's.

If you are attacked, your primary concern should be to safely escape to a more secure location. In fact, you have very few choices if you are attacked with a weapon. You can run, resist, or comply. You can always resist if compliance is not separating you from danger.

Resistance, however, should be the very last option considered. If you resist at first, it may be more difficult to change to a nonviolent compliance strategy later.

If you do choose to fight immediately, remember that you have several disadvantages. The first is that your assailant picked the location of this robbery. You are on his turf, his terms, and his schedule. He has many advantages, and you have very few. If you choose to fight, fight to escape—not to win. As soon as you have attacked, run and evade. If you are still alive at the end of a fight, you are a winner.

Whether you resist or whether you comply, you must prepare yourself immediately for escape. Stay calm. Focus your attention on your attacker. Agree to do what he wants. Tell him, "I will cooperate." Watch *him,* not his weapon. Keep your confidence up. If he says he has a weapon, ask to see it. He may be bluffing. Be willing to give up your property if he isn't.

Your property is not worth your life or an extended visit to the hospital. Separate yourself from your possessions. Give them to him. Better yet, drop them and run. If your attacker wants the money or the property more than he wants you, he will be diverted while you escape.

As long as you are talking, you are not being shot at or stabbed, so be willing to negotiate. By negotiate, I mean to discuss the crime. *Never, ever, plead or cry.* This gives the offender more power over you. Observe his behavior while you talk to him. See if you can distract him. If not, give up your property.

DURING A ROBBERY OR SEXUAL ASSAULT

- Negotiate.
- Never plead or cry.
- Observe the criminal's behavior.
- Distract him.
- Never believe what he says. He is a liar.

Whatever you do, don't believe anything your assailant says. He is a criminal and a liar. He will tell you anything to get you to do what he wants. If you are a female, he might tell you to give up your money, then take off your clothes so you can't follow him while he escapes. He might even tell you that he won't hurt you or rape you. Don't believe him—no matter what he says. If you are going to resist, now is the time. Don't let him have any more control over you than he already has. Taking your clothes off will give him more power and lessen your options.

Now is the time to fight and escape, or submit. You are the only one who knows your capability or whether you have the emotional or physical stamina to resist. Listen to your instincts, develop your avoidance skills, and cope as well as you can.

If the robber wants you to get into his car, this is the time to say no. Don't do it if you can prevent it, even if the perpetrator is threatening you with a gun. Run in the opposite direction. Run away from the direction his car is headed. A girl's chance of being raped or murdered increases considerably when she gets into a car. Her

Don't get into an assailant's car.

chances of being raped or killed on the street are fairly low. Even when a criminal has a gun, he may not want to use it. Gunfire, screams, or any other loud noise will attract attention. He doesn't want attention.

Some high-crime neighborhood residents use additional protection measures. Girls may throw their purses and run. Boys or girls may carry a "flash roll," which is actually appeasement money. Many victims use a flash roll to buy their way out of trouble. The roll includes several one-dollar bills rolled up inside a five-dollar bill. If a crackhead really wants your money, he will go after the cash while you escape. Some victims even say, "You can have the money. It's all I have." You are not going to be attacked ordinarily, though occasionally offenders are angry that they you didn't have as much money as wanted. Many street robbers will just take the money and leave. Be very careful when you escape this way however.

During a Gunfight

How should you react when you hear gunshots? First, you should drop to the ground or sidewalk. I don't care what you are wearing or how muddy the ground is. Drop immediately! Don't run. Flatten out and evaluate the situation. If you are on a sidewalk and there is a curb, try to get below the curb. Even dumpsters and garbage cans provide some protection. Crawl away from the gunshots if you can't find cover.

Most bullets are flying by at least eighteen inches off the ground. The lower you are, the better your chances of surviving. Try to pinpoint where the shooting is coming from. Sometimes hysterical people get behind cars only to discover that they are on the wrong side (they can see the shooter), or that they have stumbled into the middle of a gang fight.

Get under cover as fast as you can. Cover can be anything that will stop or deflect a bullet. Telephone poles, trees, steel Postal Service mail receptacles, concrete barriers, cars, or buildings are suitable. Even a curb or a fire hydrant is better than nothing. Concealment is somewhere to hide, like behind a hedge, but hiding won't protect you from a bullet.

If you are on foot when the gunfire starts, getting farther away is important. Most shootings occur within ten feet, rarely over twenty.[4] Criminologists J. L. Simmons and George McCall wrote that "getting (even) twenty feet away makes you twice as safe as ten feet away, and a hundred feet away is many times safer."[5]

During A Fight

What should you do during a fight? The response to this question doesn't require a lot of thought, just common sense. The only response is to leave. The fight may start with fists but end with weapons. It may also escalate into a gang fight.

I know that walking away from a fight is difficult. You want to see what happens. Johnny, the bully, is finally getting what he has deserved for years, and you want to see every punch! This is not a wise decision however. Your best safety advice is to leave.

Let's say the bully is being thoroughly defeated by a kid once considered a coward. The bully thought he was a weakling and a wimp. The wimp gained thirty pounds this year and today he's a vigilante. He's decided he isn't going to be pushed around any more. He knocks the bully down

> Leave the scene of a fight quickly. It may escalate into a gang fight or weapons may be used.

with a strong left hook. You laugh—after all, this clown has abused you too—and the bully looks up at your face just as you chuckle. It doesn't take a genius to know that when the bully recuperates, you're going to be his next victim. Don't give the bully another good reason to put you at the top of his persecution list. Leave.

Bomb Scares

Bomb threats are another reality in today's schools. Usually the threat is a vicious prank. Somebody is bored or wants the school evacuated because he is not prepared for that day's test. Ninety-nine percent of all bomb threats are hoaxes. On any given day when there is a bomb threat, the chances are that it is not a real danger.

Schools, however, must react to threats of this type to ensure the safety of every student. Usually this includes a thorough search of the school property by authorities. Sometimes firefighters, police officers, bomb dogs, and EMTs come and search as well. The best thing you can do is to follow the directions of your teachers and school administrators.

Sometimes the bomb threats are real. Several bombs were detonated at Colombine High during the deadly attack there. One of them exploded the night after the attack. Bomb squads defused several other active bombs. One of these had been placed with bags of nails, broken glass, and an egg timer around a twenty-pound propane tank. Had these bombs detonated, more students would have been maimed or killed.

If there really is a bomb, what can you do to increase the likelihood of survival? Again, the best thing you can do is to follow the directions of school authorities. If they want to evacuate, then do so in an orderly fashion. Don't rush out, but don't dawdle either. Your risk is increased whenever you speed ahead or drag behind those evacuating the area.

If I were evacuating a school and believed the threat to be true, I would prefer to be in the center of a crowd of other students. Most bomb victims are not hurt by the explosion itself. They are injured by glass and shrapnel. In a bomb threat, the worst place you can stand is adjacent to a window. If there is no alternative, then stand with your back to the window. If there are any curtains, shades, or blinds, use them. Any cover is better than none because the glass shards may blind you if you are looking toward an explosion when the windows shatter.

The hallways are safer than the classrooms, just as in a tornado drill. The building has its strongest reinforcements there.

God's Rules for Safety

The rules for crime prevention, crime avoidance, and crime deterrence continue to increase in complexity. Moving from bullies and campus criminals to bombs, glass shards, and maiming are gargantuan steps. The more complex the issue, the more you may be afraid you will do the wrong thing.

This is where faith will help you. The Lord has made many promises to those who believe in him. When Captain John Testrake's plane was skyjacked into Lebanon, he watched as a Shiite revolutionary beat a U.S. Navy diver to death right in front of him. Yet, in spite of this, Captain Testrake continued to recall Deuteronomy 31:6. "Be strong and of good courage, do not fear nor be afraid of them; for the LORD your God, He is the One who goes with you. He will not leave you nor forsake you."

You may ask: "If God is going to take care of me, why do I need to know about crime avoidance and deterrence?" You need to do everything your instincts, intellect, and knowledge tell you to do. That is why God gave human beings logical minds with the ability to reason. That is why God requires personal responsibility for all of your actions—good or bad. That is why God's message teaches character, confidence, courage, compassion, and common sense. God will protect those who believe in him. I believe that, but I don't think that God will protect me if what I do is stupid.

I work with many mission organizations all over the world. Some of the same principles in this book are taught in our missionary survival seminars. I know of many missionaries, both male and female, who have been victimized in violent crimes, rape, robbery, and murder. These are horrible consequences for those who are called to God's service. So, if a full-time missionary

or a local pastor is harmed by criminals or revolutionaries while serving God, what are your chances? I can't
answer the question, but I can show you how to do
everything necessary to avoid, deter, and prevent
crime. When I have done everything reasonable that a
trained professional can do, all I can do then is rely on
the Lord. And he has a beautiful answer for me in the
Scriptures.

> *I sought the Lord, and He heard me,*
> *And delivered me from all my fears.*
> *They looked to Him and were radiant,*
> *And their faces were not ashamed.*
> *This poor man cried out, and the* LORD *heard*
>   *him,*
> *And saved him out of all his troubles.*
> *The angel of the* LORD *encamps all around those*
>   *who fear Him,*
> *And delivers them.*
>
> *Oh, taste and see that the* LORD *is good;*
> *Blessed is the man who trusts in Him!*
> *Oh, fear the* LORD*, you His saints!*
> *There is no want to them who fear Him.*
> *The young lions lack and suffer hunger;*
> *But those who seek the* LORD *shall not lack any*
>   *good thing.*
>
> *Come, you children, listen to me;*
> *I will teach you the fear of the* LORD*.*
> *Who is the man who desires life,*
> *And loves many days, that he may see good?*

Keep your tongue from evil,
And your lips from speaking deceit.
Depart from evil and do good;
Seek peace and pursue it.

The eyes of the LORD are on the righteous,
And His ears are open to their cry.
The face of the LORD is against those who do evil,
To cut off the remembrance of them from the earth.

The righteous cry out, and the LORD hears,
And delivers them out of all their troubles.
The LORD is near to thee who have a broken heart,
And saves such as have a contrite spirit.

Many are the afflictions of the righteous,
But the LORD delivers him out of them all.
He guards all his bones;
Not one of them is broken.
Evil shall slay the wicked;
And those who hate the righteous shall be con-
    demned.
The LORD redeems the soul of His servants,
And none of those who trust in Him shall be con-
    demned. (Ps. 34:4–22)

Is this passage just some religious mumbo jumbo, or does it mean what it says? I think it means what it says. It's real—a promise I can count on. The righteous (believers) cry out and the Lord hears. The Lord delivers them from destruction. The Lord has promised to protect those who depend on him, and he made this covenant in a clear and precise manner.

Make sure that you and the Lord are in a faith partnership and that you, personally, follow his teachings and grow in grace. You do this in prayer, meditation, Bible study, and church attendance. You don't "do something for God so that he will do something for you." You do it because God loved you enough to send his only Son to die for you that you might have everlasting life. You do it because you reflect God's love back to him. You do it because Christ has changed your life forever. This is a genuine faith protective alliance, not some legalistic contract you made with God because you were afraid.

chapter 10

Rape and Sexual Assault Avoidance

Elizabeth edits the school yearbook. She frequently stays after school to work with Mrs. Jones, the English teacher responsible for the school yearbook. Late Tuesday afternoon, Elizabeth walked down the hall to use the rest room. As she was leaving, a large boy came in, blocking her way. He was gross, nasty, and rude. Using four-letter words, he told Elizabeth that he was going to have sex with her. She wanted to leave, but this big, crude monster-guy blocked the way.

Elizabeth's heart was in her throat because she was so scared. She didn't say a word but pretended compliance. Nodding, she turned and walked back toward the stalls. The ruse worked as the potential rapist vacated his vigil before the door. She saw her chance, and jerking past him, she ran! She almost made it, too, but he grabbed her from behind. Immediately he grabbed her breast with his left hand and ran his hand down her zipper with his right.

Even though it was unlikely that anyone would hear, Elizabeth began her high-intensity power yell. From deep inside her stomach and lungs, she turned the gift of sound loose in a very resourceful way. As the decibels kicked in, she also stomped her assailant's instep.

Glad that she had worn cowboy boots instead of softer rubber sneakers that day, she let him have it. As she stomped, he loosened his grasp with his right hand. Twisting just a little, she backhanded his crotch really hard, again and again. Like a drummer, she let her fist run a staccato beat!

When he screamed and released her, she ran out the door and down the hall! The guy was still there crying when the school security officer arrested him. Three days later, when Elizabeth saw him at the preliminary hearing at the county court house, he could barely walk.

Elizabeth is a successful victim. Yes, she has nightmares about this character, and he did touch her in awful ways, but she wasn't raped, and she really has a stronger self-image than ever before. In fact, her classmates gave her a nickname—Tuffe, a personal description for "tough enough."

Rape Can Happen to Anyone

The United States has the world's highest rape rate of the countries that publish rape statistics.[1] American women are several hundred times more likely to be raped than are women in other countries.[2] Our rape rate is four times higher than that of Germany, thirteen times higher than that of England, and twenty times higher than that of Japan.[3]

In fact, statisticians indicate that about one out of every four girls will be raped by the time she reaches twenty-one. A disproportionate percentage of rape victims are attacked before their fifteenth birthday, raped before they can legally drive. In fact, 29 percent of all reported rapes occur before a girl's eleventh birthday, and 32 percent occur between the eleventh and seventeenth year; thus 61 percent of all reported rapes occur before the seventeenth birthday.[4]

Over 40 percent of all rapes occur at home,[5] the one location women feel safe. When you talk about rape, you should talk about avoidance, deterrence, and prevention. By the time a rape attempt is initiated, it may be too late. In fact, rapes are so frightening that only about one-third of all victims are strong enough to say no and resist. Only about 12 percent of rape victims even try to resist in any way, and only about 12 percent try to run away.[6] Most rape victims are incapacitated by their fear, even to the point that they don't say "no," and they don't even scream.

The time to avoid rape is *before it happens.* Obey the safety and security rules set by your parents and school. Obeying the rules protects you, sets limitations on the behavior that can occur, and keeps you from having a lifetime of nightmares.

The first thing to realize is that rape can happen to you or those you love. The girls most likely to be raped are the ones who refuse to listen to good advice. They believe rape isn't going to happen to them, so they don't listen. Without this knowledge, they are much more likely to be attacked. They are in denial. "Nice girls aren't raped." "Christian girls don't get raped." "I don't have to worry. My daddy, brother, or boyfriend will look after me." "I'm too young." "I'm too fat." "I'm too skinny." "My chest is flat, and I am not attractive." "I have pimples." "My braces are as big as a car bumper." "I'm not pretty enough to be raped." "Athena over there, the one with the playmate physique, the big chest, and well-rounded hips is likely to be raped, not me."

However, this is *not* the way rapists pick victims. Rapists pick naive girls who don't think rape will happen to them. They pick somebody vulnerable and alone. They pick soft targets. They pick girls who are so lax and unaware that they probably can't identify the creep who rapes them. They pick young girls who take unnecessary risks. They don't necessarily pick the girl most likely to become a movie star or a professional model. Date rapists pick girls who believe they can always talk a boy out of their attack. By refusing to accept rape as a real possibility, most girls do not learn the PINs (pre-incident indicators).

There are three categories of girls. Some make things happen. They are assertive leaders. The second category includes the weak. Things are always happening to them. They are at risk. It's the third category, however,

---

THREE CATEGORIES OF GIRLS

- Some girls make things happen.
- Some girls discover that things are always happening to them.
- Some girls don't know what's happening. These girls are in the highest risk category.

which is alarming. *The girls most at risk are the girls who don't know what's happening.* They are naive, vacillating, and weak. From the criminal's point of view, they are good victims.

In her book, *Safe: Not Sorry,* Tanya Metaksa wrote, "If women spent as much time actually thinking about taking real precautions as they do in preparing their hair and makeup, they would find that they were ready to defend themselves against almost any kind of violence. And, by being prepared, they might even prevent a violent act."[7]

Pre-Rape Interviewing

Most rapists "interview" their victim; that is, they talk to the victim before they attack. (Often such interviews occur before assaults, robberies, or even house burglaries too.) The crooks want to know who they are dealing with, but in this particular interview, they are contemplating rape. The interview may be about anything or nothing, but it will *not* be about sex. This would make most girls feel uncomfortable, especially with a stranger. No, this guy is just trying to discover if you will be a "good" victim.

The rapist is interviewing, trying to determine your awareness level. He may ask for change, a match, or directions. He is looking to see what your boundaries are. He's testing you to see how far he can go. If he senses excessive nervousness, he knows you're on to him. In a public place, leave quickly. In a private place, start running and yelling.

Frequently the rapist will touch the girl in the interview. He'll probably touch your arm or shoulder first, or if you both are sitting, he may touch your knee. The touch won't be threatening at first, but it sets a stage for more intimate touching. Stop the touching immediately, establish your boundaries, and tell him to leave. This really establishes "your space." If he doesn't leave, then you should.

Some interviews are silent. Nothing is said. The guy watches you, looking for weakness, a heavy load, inattention, or a lack of awareness. Then he jumps you. If you are inattentive, you will never even see him watching you; nor will you witness his approach.

Pre-Rape Tests

Sometimes creeps will see how far they can intrude into your space and if they can violate your "safety circle." Often they will purposefully brush up against you to see how you will react. Most girls just move over, preferring not to make a scene. When a guy brushes up against your breasts or your hips, however, you *should* make a scene. While it is possible that this touching is accidental, especially in a crowd, a bus, or a subway, in all likelihood it is purposeful.

Think about it. Did anyone ever brush up against your breasts, touch your buttocks, or brush up against your thighs before you started to develop into womanhood? Probably not. Why do you suddenly feel uncomfortable about guys touching you? You feel uncomfortable because it's not right and it's probably not accidental.

Don't let this character think you are a docile pushover. Don't let him violate your space, and most especially, don't let him touch you. Respond in a loud voice: "Back off! Get away! Don't you touch me again." Don't move out of your space. Make *him* move by the sheer power of your words, your personality, and your assertiveness. After all, you were there first.

I know you don't think that Christian girls should be rude, but this is an exception. Don't be afraid to be rude. Your personal safety is much more important than his feelings. Remember, too, that most rapists want a victim, not a fight.

By being assertive and standing up for your rights, you decrease the likelihood that you will become a rape victim. However, in demanding your rights, do it in a ladylike fashion. He will respect you for being assertive. If you get mad and call him names or speak to him in a derogatory manner, you may actually increase your chances for a future assault or rape because you could make him angry.

By the same token, if you allow him to get too close, you are sending another silent message. "I'll be a good victim!" If you merely move away, or worse yet, remain in that location, he'll cut you off later, isolate you, and rape you. He has already learned that you'll be "safe" to attack.

Many girls choose to retreat and suffer in silence rather than making a scene. They probably believe that this is the most ladylike option. Unfortunately, this reaction is a serious blunder. Even silence can be deadly when you are looking at a predator. When you retreated, you showed him in a very clear way that he could successfully encroach upon your space and that you will be compliant. Don't make the compliance mistake. Be assertive, but not aggressive. You don't want to infuriate this creep so badly that he stalks you until he gets you.

Good posture is one of the best rape-avoidance techniques. Keep your head up and your shoulders back. I'm not suggesting you exaggerate your posture to get another inch of bustline. I'm merely talking about maintaining a positive bearing and a good posture, both of which suggest assertiveness. Self-reliant and assertive girls make terrible rape victims.

Rapists want an over-compliant couch potato. Shy, timid, fearful, weak, and young girls are much more likely to be raped. Your bearing, posture, and attitude can decrease the likelihood of rape and all other street crimes. Assertive girls are rarely raped, and then only when they make unacceptable safety choices or are defiant about reasonable rape-precautionary procedures.

Assertive girls know what to say. They communicate well. "What part of "no" don't you understand?" They are precise, direct, and appropriate to the situation. They are not afraid of being uncooperative, discourteous, or even rude to a despicable example of humanity.

School is a priority location for a rape. The National School Boards Association reported that 7 percent of the violent acts committed at school involved rape. In large urban school districts, the rate is 20 percent.[8] While many people are usually at a school during normal hours, this is not true either before or after school. Even during school, if a girl can be isolated, she can be raped.

One junior-high-school student I interviewed told me that she was attracted to a fellow classmate. He already had a girlfriend, but this teen thought she was in love. This fellow talked her into going into an unused school dressing room with him. She thought they would talk, hold hands, and maybe kiss a little. She did want a little romance, but she didn't want sex, and she certainly didn't want rape. Had she stayed in public view, she wouldn't have been attacked. She feels very guilty because she was gullible enough to follow his directions.

Pick your spots when you date, and even when you arrange a meeting. Rape can happen anywhere, but it is far more likely to happen at certain sites and times. Higher risk locations can be avoided when you do the picking.

Obeying the rules at school can help save you from the tragic consequences of this despicable act. Even with all the vulgar words you hear at school, rape is still the ugliest four-letter word in the entire English language. School grounds, school parking lots, school buildings, and sports bleachers may all camouflage the ever-present attack dangers.

Rape Myths

Your perception of a rapist is probably a myth. More than likely, you think a rapist looks dumb, is probably of another race, has heavy eyebrows, Mafia facial characteristics, and can overpower any woman. *This stereotype is misleading.* Most rapists are working-class men, doctors, preachers, and lawyers. These guys undress you with their eyes before they attack you. When they look at you inappropriately, you're getting an early warning, a pre-incident indicator (PIN).

The truth is that the rapist is normally of above-average intelligence. A large percentage are young, but many rapists are married guys with families. They come from all economic and family backgrounds, occupations, ethnic groups, and cultures.

There is also a myth of race. In the U.S., only about 20 percent of all rapes reported to the police involve people of a different race. Eighty percent of all rapists attack girls or women of their own race.[9] This tells us that you should worry more about your boyfriend, neighbor, or the boy sitting beside you in class. Stereotypes increase your risks because you avoid guys who probably won't hurt you and end up taking risks with guys who will.

Date-Rape Prevention

My wife and I have one daughter and four sons. We had high standards for Kathy and her brothers. When Kathy started dating, we wanted to know the boy, and we wanted to know his parents. On every date he was to come in and meet us. If a boy had honked from our driveway, I would have told him to leave—without Kathy. Some of you may think this is an archaic practice left over from the dark ages; but in fact, this practice is protective. Visiting with parents is not only courteous; it is a strong security approach.

I always talked to Kathy's date about where they were going, what they were going to be doing, if any adult chaperones would be at these events, and when they would return. I always let the boy know that I personally held him accountable for her safety. Kathy always had to be in by 10:30 to 11:00 PM. Kathy lived at home during her college years, and these time limits continued until she was married.

We live in a university community, and after the movie theater, the bowling alley, or the skating rink close down, it's hard to find an acceptable activity for Christian young people. In fact, getting drunk, high, or pregnant seemed to be the only late-night youth activities I could envision. Automobile fatalities related to alcohol abuse continue to spiral out of control after midnight, and violent crimes of assault, car jacking, rape, and murder increase dramatically during the early morning hours. Eleven o'clock was a good standard a decade ago, and it still is!

Date Rape

Date rape is a problem for women of all ages. The criminological literature gives a clear indication of the type of guy who will rape on a date or social occasion. In a Florida survey of young rape victims, approximately 97 percent of them knew their attackers.[10]

Rapes committed on a date or by someone you know well seldom occur without warning. There are several PINs that serve as warnings. Acquaintance rapists exhibit several forms of inappropriate behavior. Craig Huber and Don Paul state that the warnings come from his eyes, his mouth, and his hands.[11]

Taking note of eyes, mouth, and hands can save you a lot of discomfort later. When I talk about eyes, I'm not talking about the appreciative look of a boy who thinks you're pretty or who thinks your new outfit is stylish. In most cases, an appreciative look from someone you care about is flattering, especially if this is your favorite

---

THE DATE RAPIST

- Someone the victim knows.
- Does not respect your wishes.
- Makes you feel uncomfortable.
- Talks about sex.
- Attempts to isolate you, get you off alone with him.
- Tries to be romantic, first attempting seduction.
- Starts touching or pawing you when seduction is unsuccessful.
- The intensity of his attack escalates when you say "no" or try to stop him.
- Attack! Rape!

---

somebody or you're in love. The look I'm talking about is negative, cheap, tawdry, and lewd! The boy undresses you with his eyes, stares at your body, and makes you feel uncomfortable. He should be looking at your eyes, not at your breasts, hips, or thighs.

The mouth itself, what he says and the gestures he makes with it, is another PIN. Is his speech demeaning or vulgar? Does he talk about sex in a degrading way? Does he curse and use cheap four-letter words? Does every conversation revert to sex? Why does he want to talk about sex when you were talking about homework? If his compliments make you feel debased rather than flattered, then you've already keyed in on another warning.

Some date rapists are totally inconsiderate of their date's feelings. Does your date belittle you? Does he act in a dominating or hostile way toward you or other

girls? Does he act like he owns you? Is he always negative about girls? Does he treat you in a subservient
manner? Is he angry at the world? If he's full of resent-
ment, he won't be a good date anyway. Don't just go
along with what your date wants. Don't always let him
pick the movie or the restaurant or the entertainment.
You pick it.

If things work out, and you date this fellow for a
while, *then* let him choose, but don't ever be a
pushover. The real message you need to send him is
that you will not be a compliant, nonresisting victim,
and you *will* tell on him later if he touches you inappropriately or harms you in any way. Terminate any
relationship that is forceful, even if the force is psychological instead of physical. Either way, you should
know that you are going to be harmed.

If you begin to feel uncomfortable during a date,
listen to your instincts. Call your family or a friend.
Use any excuse to get away. If you don't feel safe, refuse
to ride home with him. Date rape police files are full
of examples where the victim had strong intuitive feelings that something wasn't right but failed to act on
these feelings.[12]

If you are attacked,
you can escape, submit, or
fight. Decide today what
you will do, and prepare
for this possibility. Authorities generally agree that
the sooner a girl defends
herself, the more likely
she is to avoid rape.

GIRLS WHO AVOID RAPE
• Freak out
• Get really mad
• Have a fit
• Power yell
• Run away
• Escape

Don't be afraid to resist. Girls are often injured in a rape attempt just as they are injured in resisting, but self-defense and then escape are usually the best responses in a date rape attempt. Girls who have avoided rape remember freaking out, getting really angry, going ballistic, screaming, and running; these girls avoided rape.

Every rape-avoidance activity is intended to help you escape. Even if you must fight, you fight in order to gain the opportunity to run, not to duke it out with a fool. Some girls do pretty gross things to avoid rape. Tell the hormonally influenced sex pig that you are menstruating. Stick your finger down your throat to the point of choking. Throw up! Defecate! If Johnny Romeo is pawing you and won't stop, vomit all over him. Let's see how sexy he thinks you are when he's wiping your puke off his new jacket or when he is smelling body waste on his car seat. He'll probably lose his erotic fantasy completely.

Date rapists not only have Roman hands (roaming hands) and Russian (rushing) fingers, they like to touch you a lot. Some of the touching may be acceptable, but if holding his hand or hugging him makes you feel uncomfortable, you're out with the wrong boy. Listen to your feelings. If his touch feels terrible, then you are too close. You're in trouble. Get away from him quickly. Call home, and let your folks pick you up. They will be glad to come. Then stay away from him in the future. Don't go out with him again, and tell your friends what he was like. He will continue his activities as a sexual predator until he's stopped.

WHEN THE STORM OF RAPE GETS CLOSER

- His eyes devour you.
- His mouth is out of control.
- His hands roam freely, even when you attempt to restrict his movements.

Another PIN is to beware of the boys other boys don't like. Sometimes people are misjudged, but by and large, there is a reason for most behavior. Just as girls talk to other girls and share their innermost thoughts, so do boys. If the boys feel uncomfortable around Sensual Joe Sleazeball, you should pay attention to this fact as well.

Sensual Joe probably told the boys he is "making it" with you even when he doesn't have the nerve to attempt a kiss. If you get a bad reputation, deserved or not, you're in another kind of trouble. Other guys may think you're easy. Fewer guys will accept "no" for an answer. They "know" you're sexually experienced because of the "facts" Sleazeball told them, so what's the big deal if you do it again with them?

Except in date rape, many girls think some character jumps out of a nightmare and into her life, totally surprising her. This type of rape is called *blitz rape* and is named after the German Nazi bombing of England in WWII. Though it does occur on occasion, it constitutes only a small percentage of all rapes. If he has a knife or gun, it is extremely risky to resist. If he is just using superior strength and weight to his advantage, you may choose to resist.

Watch the Men Watching You

Girls are really at risk. It's like your city or town is a war zone. You never know when the enemy will strike. He chooses when and where to attack. You can only attempt to defend yourself at that time and site and by taking pre-rape precautions. The best behavior is to stay out and away from possible rape situations. Avoid excessive risk, creepy boys, and dangerous locations, and pay special attention to the boys or men paying attention to you.

What Are You Going To Do Now?

This is an important question. You've read a lot of material. You've been shown how to be safer and more secure. You've learned the crime-avoidance and personal-survival approaches of great men of the Bible. However, the decision on whether you accept these tactics, reject these tactics, or remain complacent (because surely God will never allow something bad to happen to you) is still yours to make.

Certainly I would agree that there are no guarantees that you can always prevent any individual crime. No one can always predict everything, from the weather to a criminal attack, but you can usually predict those human possibilities likely to happen to you. Which of the possibilities is probable at your school or in your neighborhood? Decide what is likely to happen to you.

Tim Powers and Richard Isaacs, in *The Seven Steps to Personal Safety,* recommend "when/then" exercises. *When* a street assault occurs, *then* I will _____.

When a robbery attempt occurs, *then* I will _____ .
When a rape attempt occurs, *then* I will _____ .
Plan ahead. Know how you will respond. Know what you want and need. Some victims may want revenge, so a street-tough gang member may want to fight it out with his assailant. If you are an average teenager, however, you should only use such force as is necessary to escape. Survival is the final exam and the only conclusive measure of success after a criminal attack.

When You Are Attacked

When you are attacked or when you suspect an attack, you need to evaluate the situation. Then you need to respond reasonably—not too much, but not too little either. The best approaches always center around deterring or avoiding a potential crime. Reactionary steps are responses to an attack that has already begun.

As I interview older children and teenagers all over the U.S., I find that many have lost faith in the American dream. They feel threatened, isolated, and alone. Since teen violence is escalating and they are afraid, many believe the situation is hopeless. As a police and security professional, this point of view really disturbs me.

I have seen communities, public-housing developments, schools, and individuals become safe and secure even though they had experienced extraordinarily high crime rates in the past. For the last twenty years I have helped build security out of chaos and peace out of anarchy. I have even applied most of these crime-prevention methods in foreign countries where

American missionaries were targeted for robbery, rape, kidnapping, and murder. I know these methods work, but I have also become aware of the fact that very few teenagers understand crime prevention or crime deterrence. You need to understand what a "security consciousness" is all about.

Furthermore, teenagers usually aren't concerned about security until they become a crime victim. Then it is too late. The trauma, psychological fear, and personal injuries are harmful in many ways beyond the stress of the crime itself. Those most injured are the naive victims who thought that it wouldn't happen to them.

Accept the Probability of Crime

The first step toward personal safety and security is to accept the fact, even the probability, that you will become a victim before your nineteenth birthday. The next step is to plan to avoid that probability and to train yourself in avoidance techniques. To accomplish this objective, you must accept responsibility for your own security. You can't delegate it to anyone else. Mom or Dad will serve as your loving guardians; but in many cases you, personally, may be the most "streetwise" member of your family.

With information and misinformation overwhelming the average Christian, it is little wonder that parents, teenagers, and younger children just don't know what to do. The multiplicity of choices is confusing. Mr. Security (Issy Boim) wrote, "We're drowning in information and starving for knowledge."[1] With *Staying Safe at School* preparation, you don't have to be confused. Discuss your security choices, decisions, and options with your parents and other responsible adults.

Christian teenagers are overwhelmed with crime occurrences. You read and hear about so many reports that you become conditioned to them. It's kind of like cancer; almost every family has some. You expect crime, especially in poor neighborhoods; but somewhere in the recesses of your mind, you expect it to happen somewhere else, to someone else, and in another neighborhood. In spite of all the statistical data, you think you will not be victimized.

The most important thing you can do to avoid crime is to learn to be aware. Be aware of your surroundings. Be aware of the school. Be aware of the neighborhood. Be aware of who is around you, especially those approaching "your circle of safety." Let crime prevention and crime avoidance become your best and strongest habit.

Concentrating on your problems, daydreaming, or philosophical contemplation can be dangerous. A vigilant and observant attitude should become a way of life. Police officers, security agents, and soldiers reflect this attitude; they have to, or they will not survive. By walking with your shoulders squared and with an erect posture, you lower the chance that you will become a crime victim. By always looking, seeing what you observe, and interpreting your observations correctly, you can avoid victimization.

Listen to Your Feelings

You should also listen to your feelings. Intuition is your best friend. If you are suddenly frightened, then listen carefully to your feelings and do something about your fear. Don't suffer in silence. Leave! Get out of there. Don't ignore these feelings. Don't talk yourself out of them. Do not let reason or logic influence your decision. Leave.

Become a hard target, not a soft, easy target. Target hardening is a practical philosophy that decreases crime against you. It keeps your crime from occurring. Your crime is deterred when prevention and avoidance methods are accepted as a way of life. Your crime is avoided when you see the PINs and leave in time.

Your crime is avoided when you make a criminal work harder, make it more difficult for him to succeed, make yourself inaccessible and his escape more problematic. Any of these factors reduces his ability to succeed, or at least shakes his confidence level about successfully targeting you, getting away, and avoiding arrest. Decreasing *his* security increases *yours*. Increasing *his* risk, lowers *yours*. Remember: a crook, even a teenage crook, is just another business person wanting a quick return for little risk. Take away the quick return, or increase the risk, and the criminal activity is deterred.

Keep your mind on what you are doing and where you are going. Watch, look, and listen. Watch for "whos." The who might be a Gangster Disciple, a bully, a drug pusher, a MICA, or a creep. Remember that "whos" are the ones who commit crime. Watch for troublesome people. Avoid walking near them. Change directions or walk across the street.

If people are arguing, mind your own business. If there is a fight, leave as quickly as you can. Always consider alternatives for leaving quickly. Perhaps you could jump in an unoccupied taxi and get the driver to take you away quickly. Perhaps you could step onto the bus that's driving by. Perhaps you should run down the sidewalk entrance toward the subway station and leave the threat behind you. If you aren't aware, however, you will miss all of the opportunities for avoiding this threat.

Hold your head up. Keep a strong bearing and good posture. Look around, observe, and interpret what you see in terms of the daily crime news. Don't walk with your hands in your pocket, and don't carry things in your hands if you can avoid it. That's what your backpack is for. You can't defend yourself if you're encumbered with your books and your lunch. If you see something that bothers you, leave. If you must, run! If your backpack slows you down, toss it! Run as fast as you can until you get somewhere safe, like a police station or a firehouse. At night, your run might be from total darkness into a well-lighted area.

Accept the Responsibility

Accepting the responsibility for your own safety is an appropriate decision. You know that crime can occur at any time. It can occur anywhere. However, it is more likely to occur at certain locations and at specific times. Doing your homework and developing your security program are major steps. You must be able to analyze your own risk.

Accepting responsibility for your own safety takes the four Cs: character, confidence, courage, and common sense. Responsible and law-abiding Christian

> "Mr. Security" (Issy Boam) says:
> Responsibility + preparation =
> the ability to meet unexpected challenges

teenagers are careful about safety and security issues. They accept responsibility for what they do and for what they didn't but should have.

Accepting the responsibility feels good too. You don't have to worry about how the teacher, the coach, the principal, the business owner, the police officer, or other possible "guardians" are going to help. While you will use these resources where you find them, holding yourself responsible and accountable is a healthy attitude and encompasses a healthy state of mind.

After you have accepted responsibility, the next step is preparing for these possibilities or probabilities. Then you will be ready for any security challenge. You will "be prepared," just like the scout motto requires. You will be ready to face a criminal attack with more confidence than ever before.

Being Prepared Has Tremendous Benefits

By being prepared, aware, and ready, you can decrease the advantages every criminal has. If you stay aware and keep all of the security rules, you will make it difficult for a criminal to corner you, cut you off, or isolate you. If "Crazy Joe" has been stalking you, he already knows your routines, and he uses your habits to predict your next move.

By quickly changing the routine when you recognize that you are under surveillance, he will expose

"YOUR CRIMINAL" DOES HAVE AN ADVANTAGE

- He knows when he will attack.
- He knows where he will attack.
- He takes the initiative.
- He has the element of surprise.
- He acts.
- You must react and respond.

himself as your intended assailant. Doing this at a critical moment is decisive and serves to cut off the attack. You disorient your attacker. His predictions about your behavior were invalid. You escape as he hesitates.

Altering your routine suddenly is a threat to your criminal. It reduces his confidence in his ability to complete the crime. By altering your route or the time you walk to school, you make yourself more difficult to target and you complicate the method of attack. He has already planned his attack; now you are doing something he hasn't predicted, and it bothers him. Now he is more at risk. In all probability, he will break off the planned attack and target someone who is totally unaware of the surroundings or his surveillance.

You Can Impact Crime

You can impact the crime intended for you, your school, and your neighborhood. You can influence criminals, and you can influence the juvenile delinquents who are now in your age range. Let's keep them out of our schools, out of our communities, and out of our lives. Let's create an environment where their crime is unsuccessful, where they either adjust to a noncriminal lifestyle or leave.

Crime, in and of itself, destroys faith in our schools, our society, and our government. Crime destroys our faith in each other and creates a mistrust that is harmful to all relationships. Criminals threaten and intimidate us. They reduce the quality of our lives because of the fear they instill in us. Let's always recognize the criminals, the thugs, the gangsters for what they are in order that we can defeat them. We must be vigilant in our own crime-prevention programs; we must always help the police and justice authorities remove these offenders from society, placing them in the reformatories and prisons in which they belong.

Put on the Whole Armor of God

You were given the crime-avoidance approaches of prophets, disciples, and apostles. This book, nevertheless, emphasizes your personal responsibility in the battle for school and personal safety.

You must realize, however, that the school crime, violence, bullying, drug pushing, gangster, and rape issues are also spiritual. Paul said:

> *For we do not wrestle against flesh and blood, but against principalities, against powers, against the rulers of the darkness of this age, against spiritual hosts of wickedness in the heavenly places.* (Eph. 6:12)

> ## THE LORD'S WEAPONS: THE WHOLE ARMOR OF GOD
> - The waistband of truth
> - The breastplate of righteousness
> - The shoes of peace
> - The shield of faith
> - The helmet of salvation
> - The sword of the spirit, which is the word of God
>   (Eph. 6:13–17)

The crime problem is so tied up in Satan's legions that it can't be separated from spiritual issues. Drugs, alcohol, premarital sex, promiscuity, violence, theft, rape, and rebellion are all in Satan's plan.

Christ's programs are faith, hope, peace, and love. The results of these spiritual gifts are safety and earthly—as well as eternal—security. The Lord gave us several weapons.

Paul said, "Finally, my brethren, be strong in the Lord and in the power of His might. Put on the whole armor of God, that you may be able to stand against the wiles of the devil" (Eph. 6:10–11).

The issues of crime and disorder are the same in the twenty-first century as those in the first and second centuries. These issues continue to be spiritual but are expressed as crime, violence, disorder, mayhem, and rebellion. Follow the safety rules. "Children, obey your parents in the Lord" (Eph. 6:1) in all Christ-approved behavior. Conduct yourself with dignity, and others will respect you as well.

There are several ways to earn respect and they are taught in God's Holy Word. Paul gave us additional directives in Philippians 4.

Let your gentleness be known to all men. The Lord is at hand.

Be anxious for nothing, but in everything by prayer and supplication, with thanksgiving, let your requests be made known to God; and the peace of God, which surpasses all understanding, will guard your hearts and minds through Christ Jesus.

Finally, brethren, whatever things are true, whatever things are noble, whatever things are just, whatever things are pure, whatever things are lovely, whatever things are of good report, if there is any virtue and if there is anything praise-worthy—meditate on these things. (Phil. 4:5–8)

Remember, too, that in our confrontational society, "A soft answer turns away wrath" (Prov. 15:1). Sometimes an apology can extricate you from being a victim. Saying, "I'm sorry that I offended you. Please forgive me," is not demeaning, even when you've done nothing wrong or when the other person was rude, aggressive, or violent.

In the Second Letter to Timothy, Paul reminded him that athletes must follow the rules to win, soldiers must submit to their commanding officers, and farmers must work hard for a good crop. We do our best, then leave the results to God.[2]

You therefore must endure hardship as a good soldier of Jesus Christ. No one engaged in warfare entangles himself with the affairs of this life, that he may please him who enlisted him as a soldier. And also if anyone competes in athletics, he is not crowned unless he competes according to the rules.

The hardworking farmer must be first to partake of the crops. Consider what I say, and may the Lord give you understanding in all things. (2 Tim. 2:3–7)

The last advice is also spiritual. The Spanish have a beautiful way of expressing it. They say *vaya con Dios* or "go with God." When you are in the center of Christ's will, when you pray with him, walk with him, are guided by his words, and follow the crime-prevention approaches of the early Christians and the ancient prophets, you are as close to safety and security as you can be.

Vaya con Dios.

Notes

Introduction

1. Toby Jackson, "Crime in the Schools," as found in *Crime and Public Policy*, ed. James Q. Wilson (San Francisco: Institute for Contemporary Studies, 1983), 70.

2. Richard A. Fike Sr., *Staying Alive: Your Crime Prevention Guide* (Washington DC: Acropolis Books Ltd., 1994), 16.

3. Ibid., 17.

4. Ronald Stevens, *Safe Schools: A Handbook for Violence Prevention* (Bloomington, IN: National Education Service, 1995), 13.

5. James D. Brewer, *The Danger from Strangers* (New York: Insight Books, Plenum Press, 1994), 31.

6. Children's Defense Fund Press Release, April 9, 1996, 2.

7. J. Toby, *Violence in School* (Washington, DC: U.S. Department of Justice, National Institute of Justice, 1983), 32.

8. R. Craig Sautter, "Standing Up to Violence," Phi Delta Kappan (January 1995), k1–k2.

9. Brewer, 11.

Chapter 1

1. Marie Somers Hill and Frank W. Hill, *Creating Safe Schools: What Principals Can Do* (Thousand Oaks, CA: 1994), 43.

2. National School Safety Center, *Educator Public Relations, School Safety 101, 1993.*

3. Stuart Greenbaum, Brenda Turner, and Ronald D. Stephens, *Set Straight on Bullies* (Malibu, CA: The National School Safety Center, 1989), 9.

4. Richard A. Fike Sr., *Staying Alive: Your Crime Prevention Guide* (Washington DC: Acropolis Books, 1994), 100.

5. Greenbaum, Turner, and Stephens, 9.

6. National Institute of Education, *Violent Schools-Safe Schools: The Safe School Study Report to Congress* (Washington, DC: U.S. Government Printing Office, 1978), 13.

7. Nancy Day, *Violence in Schools: Learning in Fear* (Springfield, NJ: Enslow Publishers, 1996), 58.

8. Greenbaum, Turner, and Stephens, 9.

9. Arnold P. Goldstein and C. Ronald Huff, eds., *The Gang Intervention Handbook* (Champaign, IL, Research Press, 1993), 269.

10. Tim Powers and Richard B. Isaacs, *The Seven Steps to Personal Safety* (New York: The Center for Personal Defense Studies, 1993), 5.

11. Ibid.

12. M. Lawton, "Public Health Crisis: Teenage

Gun Violence," as found in *Education Week* (June 17, 1992), 14.

13. Children's Defense Fund, *The State of America's Children: 1994* (Children's Defense Fund, Washington, DC: 1994).

14. J. Gaustad, "Schools Respond to Gangs and Violence," *Oregon School Study Council Bulletin,* 34(9), 1991.

15. Children's Defense Fund, *The State of America's Children* (Washington DC: Children's Defense Fund, 1991), 42.

16. National Education Association, *Annual Report to Membership,* 1993, 13.

17. J. Toby, *Violence in School,* a U.S. Department of Justice Monograph from the National Criminal Justice Reference Service, 1983, 29.

18. National School Boards Association, *Toward Better and Safer Schools: A School Leader's Guide to Delinquency Prevention,* National School Boards Association under U.S. Department of Justice Grant Number 82-MU-AX-K045, 1984.

19. James D. Brewer, *The Danger From Strangers* (New York: Insight Books, Plenum Press, 1994), 39–40.

20. S. D. Vestermark and P. D. Blauvelt, *Controlling Crime in the School: A Complete Security Handbook for Administrators* (West Nyack, NY: Parker, 1978), 33.

21. M. R. Asher and J. Broschart, *Violent Schools-Safe Schools: The Safe School Study Report to the Congress* (as found in the *Topical Bibliography on Violence and Vandalism in Schools,* a service of the Juvenile Justice Clearing House, U.S. Department of Justice, 1978), 156.

22. Toby, *Violence in School,* 32.

23. P. M. Berra, "Study of High School Students in Five Offense Categories" Ph.D. diss., Arizona State University, 1978, as found in the *Topical Bibliography on Violence and Vandalism in Schools,* 70.

24. National School Safety Center, *Educator Public Relations: School Safety 101,* 1993.

25. Ibid.

26. The National Center for Education Statistics, *Violence and Discipline Problems in Public Schools: 1996-1997, Executive Summary,* February 1998, 2–4.

27. Alfred S. Regnery, Administrator to the U.S. Office of Juvenile Justice, "Report of Narrative Statement to the U.S. Senate Subcommittee on Juvenile Justice," (1984, January 25), 2–3.

Chapter 2

1. Donna Chaiet and Francine Russell, *In the Safe Zone: A Kid's Guide to Personal Safety* (New York: Beech Tree, 1998), 17.

Chapter 3

1. Gavin DeBecker, *The Gift of Fear: Survival Signals That Protect Us From Violence* (New York: Little, Brown and Company, 1997), 98.

2. Steven Fink, *Crisis Management: Planning for the Inevitable* (New York: American Management Association, 1986), 7.

3. DeBecker, 104.

4. Ibid., 70.

Chapter 4

1. Peter D. Blauvelt, *Making Schools Safe for Students: Creating a Proactive School Safety Plan* (Thousand Oaks, CA: Corwin Press, Inc., 1999), 1.

Chapter 7

1. Gavin DeBecker, *The Gift of Fear: Survival Signals That Protect Us From Violence* (New York: Little, Brown and Company, 1997), 69.

2. Tim Powers and Richard B. Isaacs, *The Seven Steps to Personal Safety* (New York: The Center for Personal Defense Studies, 1993), 27.

3. Ibid., 29.

4. Michael Castleman, *Crime Free: Stop Your Chances of Being Robbed, Raped, Mugged or Burglarized by 90%* (New York, Simon and Schuster, 1983), 67.

Chapter 8

1. J. Toby, *Violence in School,* U.S. Department of Justice (Washington D.C.: National Institute of Justice, 1983), 27.

2. P. M. Berra, *A Study of High School Students in Five Offense Categories,* an Arizona State University doctoral dissertation (unpublished), 1978, 70.

3. W. Landen, "Violence and Our Schools: What Can We Do?" *Updating School Board Policies,* National Association of School Boards, 23(1), 1992, 1–5.

4. Stuart Greenbaum, Brenda Turner, and Ronald D. Stephens, *Set Straight on Bullies* (Malibu, CA: The National School Safety Center, 1989), 9.

5. Arnold P. Goldstein and C. Ronald Huff, eds., *The Gang Intervention Handbook* (Champaign, IL: Research Press, 1993), 269.

Chapter 9

1. National Institute of Education, *Violent School-Safe Schools: The Safe School Study Report to the Congress,* Washington DC: Superintendent of Documents, 1978, 92.

2. A. G. Cuervo, J. Lees, and R. Racey, *Toward Better and Safer Schools* (Alexandria, VA: National School Boards Association, 1984), 12.

3. CCHR Working Group on School Violence/Discipline, *Memorandum for the Cabinet Council on Human Resources Concerning Disorder in Our Public Schools* (Rockville, MD: National Institute of Justice, National Criminal Justice Reference Service, 1984), 20–21.

4. Loren W. Christensen, *How to Live Safely in a Dangerous World* (Miami, FL: J. Flores Publishers, 1996), 116.

5. J. L. Simmons and George McCall, *76 Ways to Protect Your Child From Crime* (New York: Henry Holt and Co., 1992), 84.

Chapter 10

1. "Rape Statistics," The National Victim Center, April 23, 1992.

2. J. L. Simmons and George McCall, 76 *Ways to Protect Your Child From Crime* (New York: Henry Holt and Co., 1992), 157.

3. "Rape Statistics," The National Victim Center.

4. *Rape in America: A Report to the Nation,* by The National Victim Center and the Crime Victim's Research and Treatment Center, 1992.

5. National Institute of Law Enforcement and Criminal Justice, *Forcible Rape: Police Volume I* (Washington DC: U.S. Government Printing House, 1977), 19.

6. Ibid.

7. Tanya K. Metaksa, *Safe, Not Sorry* (New York: HarperCollins, 1997), xviii.

8. Nancy Day, *Violence in Schools: Learning in Fear* (Springfield, NJ: Enslow Publishers, 1996), 58.

9. Lee H. Bower, "Women As Victims: An Examination of the Results of the L.E.A.A.'s National Crime Survey Program," as found in *Women and Crime in America* (New York, NY: McMillan, 1981), 164–65.

10. M. Lang, "Date Rape: A Fear Many Teens Live With," *Tallahassee Democrat,* January 25, 1993, 150.

11. Craig Huber and Don Paul, *Secure From Crime,* (2nd ed.) (Woodland, CA: Path Finder Publications, 1993), 110.

12. Simmons and McCall, 153.

Chapter 11

1. Issy Boim, *Fighting Terrorism: The Security Connection for Family Protection* (Saline, MI: Safe Flyer Joint Venture Partners, 1997), 10.

2. Gwen Rice Clark, "Both Sides Needed," a devotional for March 4, 2000, found in *The Quiet Hour* (Cook Communications Ministries, March, April, May 2000), 12.